**wellcome
collection**

This book accompanies the exhibition *Play Well,*
on at Wellcome Collection from 24 October 2019 to
8 March 2020.

Play Well makes the case for play as an essential
tool, crucial for both children and wider society.
Through a wide range of exhibits *Play Well* explores
the importance of play in developing and refining
character traits, as a central tenet of education, and as
a language to express emotions and build empathy.
The exhibition examines the ways in which children's
play both reflects and adapts to the world around
them. Playground games and toys echo shifts in wider
society, while opportunities for play are limited by
concerns about risk. In light of these influences the
exhibition asks: how can we all play well?

**wellcome
collection**

Wellcome Collection is a free museum and library that aims to challenge how we think and feel about health. Inspired by the medical objects collected by Henry Wellcome, it connects science, medicine, life and art. Wellcome Collection exhibitions, events and books explore a diverse range of subjects, including consciousness, forensic medicine, emotions, sexology, identity and death.

Wellcome Collection is part of Wellcome, a global charitable foundation that exists to improve health for everyone by helping great ideas to thrive, funding over 14,000 researchers and projects in more than seventy countries.

wellcomecollection.org

Michael Rosen's Book of PLAY!

P

PROFILE BOOKS

wellcome collection

First published in Great Britain in 2019 by
Profile Books Ltd
29 Cloth Fair
London EC1A 7JQ
www.profilebooks.com

wellcome
collection

Published in association with Wellcome Collection
Wellcome Collection
183 Euston Road
London NW1 2BE
www.wellcomecollection.org

Copyright © Michael Rosen, 2019
Illustrations by Charlotte Trounce
Design by James Alexander, Pete Dyer and Sinem Erkas

The publishers would like to extend their thanks to Katharine Ailes and Sarah Goodman.

1 3 5 7 9 10 8 6 4 2

Printed and bound in Great Britain by
Clays Ltd, Elcograf S.p.A.

A CIP catalogue record for this book is available from the British Library.

ISBN 978 178816 1909
eISBN 978 178283 5189

The paper this book is printed on is certified by the © 1996 Forest Stewardship Council A.C. (FSC). It is ancient-forest friendly. The printer holds FSC chain of custody SGS-COC-2061

Contents

Introduction

(Actually, let's not call this an 'introduction', let's call it 'Hello'. I'll start again. Forget that I called it 'Introduction'. That didn't happen.)

Hello

Hello reader.

I don't know you, but the thing about a book is that it's a kind of game between the writer and the reader. This is how you play it: I sit on my own imagining what kinds of things might interest you. I conjure up books I've read and scan them in my mind for strange, funny, weird, intriguing, sad things. I conjure you up and imagine you opening this book, wondering if there is anything here that will amuse you or get you to think in a new way. Or perhaps you're the kind of person who wants knowledge. Or perhaps you're the person who wants to play.

All that was me playing with the idea of what I'm doing writing this book. Writing is a kind of play.

And if you're still reading, you're playing too. When you sit down to read, you agree to play a game. There aren't exactly what I'd call 'rules'; there's more a set of things we do that are more like the 'how to cook' part of recipe books – how to cook a book, if you like. You cook a book by doing things like picking it up – rather than throw it in the river, say. You open it up – rather than sit on it, say. If you are reading the page to yourself, you pass your eyes along the lines from left to right, rather than round and round, say. If this book was in Arabic or Hebrew, you'd be passing your eyes from right to left. If it was in traditional Chinese, you'd be passing your eyes down and up and down. If you're listening to the book, you've got your ears focused on the sounds of words, rather than on the dog that's barking outside. And as you do these things, your mind is playing. It's playing with meanings. When you read the word 'book', I'm pretty sure a dictionary didn't fly into your mind and there was a definition of 'book' sitting there. What happened was that all the times you've met the word 'book' and you've seen, heard, smelled or read a book rolled into what we might call a 'cloud of meaning'. That's your own cloud of meaning. Quite a bit of your cloud of meaning of 'book' is very similar to millions of other people's. But some of it is your very own special, personal cloud of meaning full of your own memories, feelings and sensations.

So, we're playing. Me and you.

In this book I will ask you questions. But what's the point? In real life, I ask someone a question because I want an answer. If I ask you questions in a book, and you answer them, I won't get to hear the answer. So there must be another point to me asking you questions. What would that be?

Well, I'll leave you to play with that one and I'll get on with the asking. Have you done any playing this week? (I've played 'How much of the dishwasher can I empty without breathing?' This is where I try to clear a whole deck of the dishwasher holding my breath. When I was a boy, my brother and I used to try to get from the loo to the kitchen before the sound of the flushing had stopped while holding our breath.)

Have you done a puzzle? (I tried to do the crossword in the *Times Literary Supplement*. When I do this, I usually get about five clues all by myself, and then I start cheating by using the internet to look up possible answers.)

Have you done some kind of exercise thing – star jumps, riding a bike, going for a walk – where you started off doing it by the rules but then you began to make up your own?

(I've started using the step-counter on my phone because someone told me that I'm supposed to walk 10,000 steps a day. In the middle of doing one thing, I now do crazy little walking journeys to and fro across a room. Or, in the middle of my son's 'Megs' game, I suddenly walk off, go round and round five times and come back to 'Megs'. He's not well pleased by that.)

Have you been clearing out an old room, or clearing a shelf, and found an old game and decided that you'd stop doing what you were supposed to be doing so that you could play your old game for a while? I've just moved office and I found an old 'bagatelle' board (it's a bit like pinball without any of the electric automatic stuff). I stood there flicking the marbles round the board. Actually, it made me sad. It reminded me of playing the game with Eddie, my son who died. Then I remembered that games and play are not only what you do right now, but that we each have histories of play in our minds. Layers and layers of it, sitting there, memories of great times messing about, winning, losing, arguing, trying things out – and this all feeds into the kind of person we are, how we think of what's around us. Is the world we meet something we can play with, or something that we take as a thing that's given to us?

Have you picked up a pen or pencil or felt-tip at any time this week and doodled? I doodle.

Here is a doodle that I did on Tuesday. What do you think?

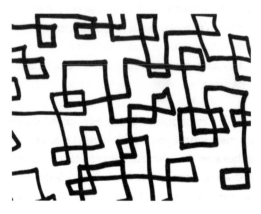

Most of my doodles are variations on this pattern. I draw repeated right angles and parallel lines till I make a pattern of different-sized rectangles and lines. Over my life I must have done thousands of these. I never keep them. I doodle away for a few minutes and then put it to one side. I sometimes do these doodles when I'm thinking of something else: such as waiting for the right word to turn up in a poem I'm writing. I've never really thought why I do them. I just know that I do.

I like my own made-up little rules that I've imposed on myself: I mustn't do curves, or diagonals; I mustn't take my pen off the page. I like the mix of order and chaos that results from my doodles. They look higgledy-piggledy, the rectangles are never made up of perfect right angles, but I can see a hidden order in them, created from the rules that I created. In a way, as I draw them, I create little problems for myself: where can I go next that will set up a new space to make a rectangle?

You could doodle all over my doodle if you like.

Have you got any felt-tips? You could colour in some of the spaces. You could make up some rules about which spaces you're allowed to colour in and which ones you can't. Or you could do tiny pictures in some of the spaces as if they are windows, perhaps.

Actually, while I'm suggesting that you could doodle on my doodle, let me suggest you could think of this whole book as a doodle. Whenever you think of something as you're reading it, you could draw or write on the book. That's a way of using play to make a book your own. Instead of treating it as a book of instructions or of knowledge that you must learn, you can treat it as something you're *having a conversation* with. If you were to write 'I disagree' or 'What about crocodiles?' in the margin, it wouldn't be rude, because I won't ever get to see it. Make the book yours by playing with it. I've been putting notes and arrows and little faces all over my books (not other people's!) for years. It's part of how I learn and remember things.

As well as playing with pen and paper, on Thursday my son got me out into our garden to play football. I've always found it fascinating that when we say that word – 'football' – it means so many different things. There are, of course, the highly organised, rule-given matches, as played by professional and amateur eleven-person teams in leagues and in schools. Aside from these, millions of people take a ball on their own, or in pairs, or in groups, or in crowds, and kick it about according to the rules that they make up to suit the place, the number, age and skills of the people. In my time, I've played one-a-side, a game we made up called 'football tennis', competing for numbers of 'keepy-uppies', 'three goals and in', games that use the wall of the playground to cannon off and so on. I've played on beaches, in parks, on playgrounds, in fields, in living rooms, bedrooms, kitchens, tents. I've played blow football on tables using a straw and ping-pong ball, with goals made out of books. I've played flick football with peas on the table until Mum shouted at me for covering the floor with peas and treading them flat. With my son, we mostly play a game where I stand with my back to a goal and he has to get past me with the ball at his feet. If I get the ball off him, I try to turn and shoot into the goal behind me. He tries to dive in and block me. If he kicks the ball between my legs, he shouts 'Megs!'

(That means a 'nutmeg' – rhyming slang for 'leg' – itself a way of playing with words!) There are no scores, and no end point – apart from my tiredness. He keeps improvising new tricks while I try to keep up with them. I cheat and grab hold of him. He becomes indignant. I tell him that he'll face worse in a real game. And on it goes. We adopt and adapt clichés from TV commentaries as we play: 'great counter', 'think of every ball as an opportunity', 'come back for the second phase', we say. We call out some of the football chants we hear on the terraces. We have fun, we yell, we pant. There is no fixed outcome, no winners or losers – though one of us may claim to have won 183-nil.

These are two very different forms of play – on my own with pen and paper, or in the garden with my son, getting sweaty and out of breath.

So, I'm thinking that maybe it would help to define play a bit. I want you to look away from the book for a moment again. Say the word 'play' and close your eyes (out loud if you're not somewhere it would sound too weird). What immediately springs to mind?

I expect a lot of you will have come up with very different ideas – because 'play' is incredibly hard to define. One problem here is that we use the word 'play' to mean very different things: we go to see 'plays' in a theatre, highly trained, highly paid sportspeople 'play' matches according to elaborate rules overseen by referees, we 'play' commercial games like Monopoly, we 'play' computer games and with older technologies we used to 'play' records, CDs and DVDs.

The kind of play I'm going to talk about in this book is more informal and free-form than that, for the most part. There will be fewer (or no) rules handed down to the players (that's you). The kind of play we're going to embark on will be giving you, the reader, the player, opportunities to invent, improvise, adapt, be creative with the world around you and with the world inside your own head. Our play will not be about competition; there will be no winners or losers, though I will admit there are times when, just for fun, you can be a teeny bit competitive, just for laughs. (If you like, you can think of this as a failing in me. Some people have said to me, 'Yeah, yeah, Mike, you say you like all this free play stuff, but actually you are quite competitive.' And I say, 'No, I'm not,' and then go away and think, Mmm, maybe they're right. That's been quite painful admitting that to you in public. Well, writing this book is supposed to be play, so that was me playing with the idea of whether it's OK to make free play a bit of a contest. Sometimes.)

Anyway, on with the book. The key thing is that you cannot fail at this type of play, although you can succeed. You can't fail, but you can succeed. That's what people call a 'saying' or an 'aphorism'. I like words like 'aphorism'. Aphphphph ... or ... ism.

With this aphorism in mind, I want to define the kind of play in this book largely as 'trial and error with no fear of failure'. By 'trial and error' I mean that not only do we not know what's going to happen ('the outcome') but the outcome doesn't really matter very much. It's the play that's important, not the result. In fact, there may well not be a result, or it may be something entirely unexpected ... or the result is something you can't measure and yet it goes into your mind and helps you become the person you are. Mysterious?

Over the next 270-odd pages (it's OK, you don't have to read every page and I promise I'm not setting you a test to find out what you've read), we are going to delve down into the deep history of play – as far back as our caveman ancestors, the spectacular and strange wonders of Ancient Egypt, the bizarre world of Surrealism, right up to the modern day – and how we can bring this rich history to bear on how we play today. We will explore several different types of play – and you, the reader, are going to get plenty of chances to be involved. Each chapter will include a handful of prompts and ideas for how you could get an extra dollop of play in your life.

Will it be fun, I hear you say? Clearly, a central point to all this is pleasure. Without pleasure we don't play. When we get fed up, annoyed, distressed or bored by play, we stop. That's because somehow when there's no pleasure, it's stopped being play. It's become something else, like a 'duty' or simply 'boring'. I think this pleasure aspect is central to play, but in saying this, I'm not saying that play is not important. Too often we think of things that make us laugh, or which are fun to do, as being not very significant or having very little value. But in this book I'm going to make the case that play, while enjoyable, is far from trivial.

Let's flip this on its head. I have another question for you.

Have you ever been bored?

If the answer is no, I say to you 'Congratulations' (or in Yiddish, one of the languages of my parents – and a language I love playing with – 'Mazeltov' (pronounced 'muzzle toff'). If you have never been bored, you are most probably utterly unique in the entire history of the human race.

Most of us experience, fairly often, that moment of 'stasis', a moment-in-between, a blankness that has an end but no exact time limit for that end. Boredom, in other words.

In our modern world we fight against boredom – after all, we have so many tools at our disposal to fend it off: the ever-present phone, the limitless landscapes of the internet, the million and one channels on TV. The time 'in between' is called 'liminal', and I believe that this 'liminal' space and time for boredom are crucial for developing our ability to experience the world in its full, Technicolor glory. It is in the moments of boredom that play is born; these are the all-important, empty, in-between times when our basic needs take a back seat, allowing a space in which we can experiment and develop creatively. As both adults and children, do you think we allow ourselves less and less of this open, 'pointless' time? I think so, and yet it is in this time that the mind can freewheel, new connections are made, new ideas are born.

So next time you're bored, rather than reaching for your phone, take a moment, lift your head and look for potential in the objects and words you see. Boredom breeds inspiration – and 'inspiration', literally, means to breathe in. So take a moment and breathe in the world around you and think of the world as something that you can play with.

(Hey, imagine for a moment that you could breathe in the world. I wonder if there's an ancient myth where a crazy malevolent god or giant breathes in the world and all the other gods complain, 'Hey, man, look what you've done!' So this giant god, says sorry and blows the world out his nose ...)

You may be a bit afraid that you have 'forgotten how to play'. I promise you, you have not. Play does not require you to be a creative genius (although it may help you become one); this book will look at how we use the world around us (which, again, I promise you, is an even more limitless resource than the internet) to encourage play.

(If you're getting cross that I keep promising you things, just cross out 'I promise'.)

Over the course of the book we will be building a tool kit to help us engage with the world in exciting, innovative and playful ways. The materials are already there at our fingertips. This book will not necessarily tell you 'what to do', but will help you develop new mindsets that give you a fresh take on the world and how you can interact with it.

We will also be looking inwards, to our vast and private inner landscapes, and discussing how we can access these in playful ways. I'm pretty keen on this idea of our inner landscapes. Why should we leave it to others to tell us what's there? We can think of ourselves as explorers of the mind, or archaeologists of our memories, picking up stuff in there, turning it over, playing with what it's there for and what we can do with it.

So, why do we do play? How does it work? What constitutes play? Play often uses objects in unexpected ways: toys, balls, bats, bikes, along with found 'stuff' like stones, twigs, bags, old clothes, plants, food, utensils, tools. Then, play often uses bits of this stuff in improvised games, little dramas and make-believe situations. Play can focus on any part of the body – and that includes our voices and how we make sounds, how the body can move, stretch, jump, crouch, lie down, spring up and the like. Play can ask our bodies to move to rhythms, pulses and any sound we find or change or play with. Play can be part of complicated processes that are part of life: cooking, cleaning, sorting, gardening, using computers and tablets. Play can be part of education, where it can enable learning to take place. Play can rehearse or 'play out' our psychodramas, the big emotional events of our lives, love, bereavement, loss, anger, rivalry, envy, death and many, many more.

One argument is that play helps us cope with change and learn flexibility. No one individual is in charge of their destiny, and a playful outlook can be very helpful with this. Our lives, our 'fates', are always wrapped up with the fates of others, whose lives are constantly changing too. We are in a continual state of flux, and the one and only certain thing about us is that we change! Our bodies are changing all the time, as are the bodies of those around us. Events and inventions are happening around us – near or far. The organisations we live, play and work in are changing. The social order that we slot into (or kick against or resist) changes. Our well-being in our living space, the amount of money that we have or don't have, the amount and kind of food we have, are all constantly changing. Where we live and who we live with, or near, changes. New people are born. People we know and love die.

We have to deal with this quite mind-boggling level of change every single day – and while for the most part we are very good at it, there are times when it feels overwhelming, we feel stress or anxiety, or even fear. How do we learn to cope with this? There is no subject at school called 'Change' (Hey! Why not?!), where we could study, play, improvise and think about change. We are expected to learn how to cope with change as we go along, or – apparently – we are supposed to amass enough knowledge from school and college to enable us to survive and flourish through all the changes going on in the world. This is a big ask. Do chunks of formal knowledge help us cope with, say, the death of a loved one? Does it help us cope with a nearby block of flats, with people we know inside, burning down? Does it help us cope with new technologies that revolutionise how we communicate with each other and all the sudden problems that arise from that? Does it help us cope with a new social movement that overturns everything we thought we knew about male and female identity? Does it help us cope with bullying? Does it help us deal with a stranger who suddenly comes into our lives and seems to have power over us? Does it help us deal with that sense that we are never good enough? Or those times when, as the song says, 'sometimes I feel like a motherless child?' Does it help us if we find – whether as a result of an accident, illness or our genetic make-up – that there are things we can't do or can't do as well: see, hear, walk, run, lift or bend? Or with a new job, moving to another country or meeting a new partner?

One argument for play, then, is that it teaches a flexibility to face up to and deal with the things on that list – or, at the very least, helps us live with change, to enjoy it and use it, to have an overall more fulfilling experience. Being in play, being in the state of mind that says, 'I wonder what might happen if I tried this' and then not worrying or being afraid of the outcome, is a state of mind that can cope with the unexpected.

It can also teach us that we can change the rules. We may not even recognise that rules are things that other humans, just like ourselves, make up. We may not know that tomorrow and the day after, and the day after that, contain within them moments that are full of possibilities. Tomorrow is not a fixed, permanent staging post. Nor is Tuesday. Nor is next Friday. Nothing is fixed, and everything is full of potential.

I realise that this runs totally counter to the way we are told that the world works.

What I'm saying here, you see, is that play can create new order. 'Order' is structure, organisation, pattern, a classification. It's the opposite of chaos. When we describe play using words like 'free' or 'improvisation' or 'experiment', it hides how through inventiveness we often create, develop, use and adapt order – breaking down the existing structures of knowledge or skill, the sequences that hang together or make some kind of sense – and re-shape them into new structures. So play gives us both adaptability and order. Through play we may discover that an object, an activity, a relationship, a situation or a social circumstance can be changed, reorganised or reordered.

Does that sound promising? Tempting? I hope so.

To talk of play with the one word (as I have here) also hides the incredible diversity of play around the world, across cultures, across time and across ages of people. Play is a part of how we develop as a society – and in this we can learn from our ancestors, some of whom we will be visiting in these pages. In my own lifetime I've seen games that I played for hours and hours – like five stones, shove halfpenny and hula-hoop – decline while other crazes and games have risen.

How come? Why do some things stay the same and other things change?

These variations and differences tell us that play is part of culture. What is culture? Culture is, in short hand, 'how we do things' – like how we sing, dress, eat, dance, do our hair, gesture and, of course, how we speak and write. Play sits in and among these things, as part of how we define ourselves, how we take part in society. By exploring it and understanding it we get an insight into what kind of people we are.

Our concept of play in the West is often bound up with the idea that play is inseparably connected to childhood, while adulthood is connected to seriousness and responsibility. Yes, we change as we grow older and develop – but all that this means is that how we play should change and develop with us. In fact, I believe play is key to helping us develop and reach our full potential. So, I don't care how old you are, you might be seven or seventeen or seventy or 170. What I do know is that however old you are, you are not too old to play. And you are not too old (or too young) for this book.*

* I'm imagining someone aged 170 picking up this book and saying, 'Hey, this looks interesting.'

Do you think one day people will live to 170? If it happens, one of the reasons will be because scientists and doctors used their knowledge and played with genes, blood, bones, brains and cells and found ways to make them work in new ways. Just saying.

Play is an intrinsic part of being human. Children we see around us don't need to be taught to play, but has this always been the case? Did our far-off ancestors, cave-dwellers, nomads, hunters, gatherers, play? Well, yes, they did. While it's not easy to trace a history of play, we do have a history of art that traces all the way back to those forebears, and this forms a physical archive of play from our earliest beginnings. It gives us a timeline that we can see, read and touch, showing how humans have played through the ages.

Play is at the heart of creativity, music, dance, song, poetry and art – it is a form of experimentation that loosens the often rigid boundaries of our very structured world, allowing us to try, allowing us to fail, allowing us to see that success might come in an unexpected shape, colour, sound or configuration. And out of this play, or through this play, we create art.

Let's delve back in time and see how it all came about.

Flutes and Figurines

So, when did it all start?

Excavations in the summer of 2008 in caves near Ulm, in the Swabia region of Germany, resulted in the unearthing of the oldest near-complete bone flute ever found, alongside an ivory female figurine carved from the tusk of a mammoth. Carbon dating suggests these artefacts are over 35,000 years old. The maker of the flute carved the instrument from the radius bone of a vulture; it is a beautiful, refined and useful instrument, much like our modern-day violins or tubas, and demonstrates intricate and skilled work.

What does this tell us?

It tells us that our forebears made music. It tells us that in the very earliest stages of our evolution, over countless years and generations, humans played with the materials they found around them – bones, rocks, sticks – discovering whether they could or would make sounds. People experimented to find out what sounds they could extract from these items, and the range of melody, rhythm, pitch and volume that the materials could offer.

People must have noticed that blowing into the different-sized tubes and cavities found in plants, bones and shells produced different sounds or 'notes'. And that where there were holes in these tubes and cavities, this too affected the note. Further play would reveal that 'stopping' and 'unstopping' the holes meant you could control these notes with your fingers. At some point people must have experimented and discovered that the process could be much improved by working on the right kind of tube, like the radius bone of a vulture or the tusk of a mammoth. And so, through play, these raw materials became instruments, and this experimentation became entertainment, ceremony and pleasure.

What inspired them to play in this way?

Was it simple curiosity? Was it 'suck it and see'? 'Have a go at that and see what happens'? It must have been a long process, full of things not working, breakthroughs, set-backs, duds. But there was no defined goal, no standard they might fail to meet; it was trial and error without fear of failure. Let's call it, playing in order to play.

And what does this tell us?

Astonishingly, over 35,000 years ago, when we might have thought our ancestors were just walking about grunting and hurling rocks at passing animals, they were in fact playing with the world around them; they were developing as artists and musicians who created instruments, music, statues and ceremonies. Isn't that exciting? Play with that idea in your mind now, conjure up a picture of your great-great-great-great (and a whole lot more great-) grandparents, in a cave in Swabia, playing with an old tusk and a sharpened rock. What would you have carved if you'd been there?

Readymade Musical Instrument

Nearly everything around you makes a sound if you tap it.
Some things that you tap might break – like the very old
glass inherited from your great-grandmother. Don't tap it.
Some things that you tap might complain – like your mother.
Best to ask first. So: find something that it's OK to tap.
Think of a rhythm: two little taps, followed by a big tap:
one-two THREE, one-two THREE. You're making music!

Ever blown air over the top of an empty glass bottle?
Get it right and it makes a noise like a flute.

Turn your saucepans upside down
and create a drum kit.

Any plastic bottle can become a bongo drum. Fill it with
stones or dried peas and you have maracas. How about
getting a group and see if you can make music together?

Because this is a book on play, I think I'm allowed to take a short detour. Bear with me. Whenever I read or say 'Swabia', a big man called Horst immediately springs to mind. I met Horst in 1957 in Germany when I was eleven, and he taught me a folk-song about a Swabian train. So one moment I'm thinking about the ancient Swabian flute and the next second I'm thinking of Horst and his 'Schwäbschen Eisenbahn' and all of us joining in with the 'chuff chuff chuff' of the chorus ... This leap of association, not quite random but certainly not logical, is an example of the many such loops and connections that we often find our brains making and which are the very permutations that allow us to play with ideas and thus come up with new ones. These associations are, in fact, an example of our brains 'playing', and this is exactly what enables us to make so many different kinds of art.

Let us take, for instance, one famous example of a surprising juxtaposition. When the painter Pieter Bruegel depicted the Greek myth *The Fall of Icarus*, he captured Icarus at the very moment he fell into the sea. We see Icarus's legs sticking out of the water. But even though Icarus and his fall are in the title of the piece, his legs are a small detail in the background. In the foreground a man is ploughing a field. In the Greek myth there is no mention of a man ploughing a field while Icarus fell to his death. This happened in Bruegel's imagination. At some point he has juxtaposed ploughing with this epic death. Is he reminding himself and us that tragedy happens while we go about our everyday business? Or is he saying that, whatever happens to that person over there, we have to get on with the daily grind of putting food on the table? Or is his point something else entirely? The viewer is left to play with these questions, engage their own imagination and become a part of the creative process of interpretation.

The play of art gives us a space to toy with ideas and feelings and to move freely between them, forming new connections. In just one page I have travelled from ancient caves filled with flute music 35,000 years ago to a German folk song in 1957, and on to Bruegel's painting of c.1558, which itself plays with an ancient myth ... And from Bruegel we might just as well leap to Anne Sexton's poem 'To a Friend Whose Work Has Come to Triumph', for good measure. I like the way the arts invite us to mess about in ideas and art of the past, asking questions. The Russian poet Anna Akhmatova did just that too with her poem 'Lot's Wife', where she reimagines a story from thousands of years ago from the Bible: the wife of a man called Lot must not look back towards the city she is leaving, but she does and is turned into a pillar of salt! The poet asks, 'Who will grieve for her?' Indeed. Who will? Akhmatova says that she will. Anyone else? The poem asks.

That's how the mind at play works.

The Wonder of Play

We have travelled back to the earliest known origins of humans playing and thus creating art. But what about the origin of the individual impulse? What was Bruegel doing when he set about with easel and paintbrush? What are the songwriters doing? What are the poets doing? And when it comes to it, what are we doing when we go to see the Bruegel? Or when we sing songs together, or read a poem?

One of the first and greatest people to think about what art and literature are for and what we 'do' with them was the Ancient Greek philosopher and scientist Aristotle. For Aristotle, the key to art's 'purpose' can be found in the word thaumazein, which is usually translated as 'wonder', as in this passage from his Poetica:

> Wonder needs to be produced in tragedies, but in the epic there is more room for that which confounds reason, by means of which wonder comes about most of all ...

You'll notice here that he seems to be contrasting 'wonder' with 'reason' – the former grows where the latter is 'confounded' – which means 'confused' or 'perplexed'. And crucially, wonder making reason confused is seen to be a good thing. We often express reason as 'rational thought', 'logic', the formation of cause and event, using the techniques of 'if this, then that ...' or 'if not this, then that ...'. Or we might assemble 'evidence' and 'come to a conclusion'. We seek to 'explain' things and 'weigh up' logically. We look for causes and come up with phrases like 'necessary or sufficient conditions'.

'Wonder' expresses two important and interrelated forms of human thought. It is something freewheeling, involving a mix of admiration, amazement, reflection, surprise, intuition – and the play of the mind. When we admire something, we might say it's 'wonderful'. But we would also use it when we are thinking about things that may or may not happen – we say, 'I wonder if ...' We are considering possibilities, and playing with them.

Have you ever heard a small child play the endless game of 'What if'? What if the sea and sky swapped places? Or what if we had legs for arms and arms for legs? Considering, wondering, is a form of play, and as we grow up we change how we use it, but it never completely disappears. When we are older, we continue to use this skill to play with possible outcomes, without tying ourselves to a finished conclusion or a definite fact. Wonder leaves us plenty of room to manoeuvre.

In his novel *Hard Times*, Charles Dickens recognised our constant struggle between wonder and reason and exploited it dramatically. Dickens's character the educator Mr Gradgrind (does he 'grind out graduates', Dickens's playful name asks?) believes that all we need in the world are facts. He keeps repeating this over and over again. On one occasion a child begins to say, 'I wonder...' and Mr Gradgrind interrupts her and commands, 'Never wonder!'

Makeshift Art Gallery

What things near you can look like something else? Two bottle-tops, the bottle opener and the corkscrew arranged on a plate – you've got a face! Hunt indoors and outdoors for unusual objects to display in your very own art gallery. Invite friends and family over to view the collection and explain what makes each one a work of art – the more ostentatious the claim, the better!*

*Hint: giving your 'art work'
a title can often help.

In Gradgrind's world there is no time or purpose for the speculation and feeling expressed in that word. For him, reason is always superior to wonder, as in the following passage:

> Herein lay the spring of the mechanical art and mystery of educating the reason without stooping to the cultivation of the sentiments and affections. Never wonder. By means of addition, subtraction, multiplication, and division, settle everything somehow, and never wonder. Bring to me, says M'Choakumchild, yonder baby just able to walk, and I will engage that it shall never wonder.

In the two millennia that passed between Aristotle and Gradgrind something happened, shifting us from a civilisation that valued wonder to one that began to regard what Dickens calls 'the cultivation of sentiments and affections' as a waste of time. This was epitomised in the Industrial Revolution, which had dominated the fifty years before the publication of *Hard Times*. This was a time of huge creativity and invention – new ways to get metal out of rocks, new forms of power to drive machines, new machines for travel and turning raw materials into clothing. Yet the idea that cultivating sentiments was a bad idea may have been in part due to the rise and success of the layer in society once called the 'middling sort' who achieved their status through all the activity of the Industrial Revolution: trade, industry and industriousness, where reason and results led to success and wealth.

But while attitudes may have shifted, play and wonder were never fully cast aside, and tellingly they simply could not be erased from our civilisation but soon emerged again in various startling new forms.

Dickens was in his own way part of the movement in art, literature and music that we call 'Romanticism', which began to flourish in the late eighteenth century and prioritised imagination, inspiration, spontaneity, freedom and the wildness of nature in contrast to the prevailing values of reason, artificiality, industrial production, money-making, exploitation and the 'city'. The poetry of, say, Wordsworth, Coleridge, Shelley, Keats and Byron, Anna Laetitia Barbauld, the novels of the Brontë sisters, the music of Beethoven and Schubert and the paintings of Constable and Turner and a later Romantic writer like Christina Rossetti all express different aspects of these ideas.

Our ideas about play today owe a good deal to the Romantics. I mentioned earlier the idea that we can think of play as being 'liminal', that it can be thought of as a kind of 'in-between' activity, occupying the space between, let's say, earning some money and going to bed, or in the holiday between one bout of working and another. By describing play in these terms, I am borrowing something from the Romantics, whose art and ideas called on people to reject or turn away from the sordid matter of 'getting and spending', as Wordsworth put it. Instead, in his poems he invites us to look at nature – the sea, the wind, the moon and the flowers ... Play has long been associated with nature in opposition to 'work'; play, like nature, is something that is not formalised and does not obey the rules of 'getting and spending' that have come to dominate society. The idea that art and play are an 'escape', then, stems to a great degree from the Romantics.

I Name This, 'Art'

Of course, the Romantics' fixation on nature and the untamed is just another chapter in the long history of play in art. One of the most playful chapters in the history of art arose in the early twentieth century in France.

In 1917 the French-born artist Marcel Duchamp bought what we might call a one-man urinal and submitted it to the Society of Independent Artists in New York – as an art work called *Fountain*, by 'R. Mutt'. This kind of 'conceptual' art is so familiar to us today, that it's easy to lose sight of the surprise, humour and playfulness involved here. For hundreds of years art had been put on a pedestal – literally and metaphorically. It had to be beautiful: the most refined form of culture that human beings could produce. It was praised as 'elevating' us to fine and noble thoughts. And here was someone suggesting that a toilet was art.

This was the beginning of a movement that would play not just with the representation of art but with the very concept of art itself: Dada.

The name itself is an example of playfulness with language. There is no consensus on where the name sprang from –

perhaps from the French word for 'hobby horse' (a child's toy), or perhaps from the nonsense syllables a child might make when playing with words (try it: da da da da, dee dee dee!), or perhaps it simply has no meaning at all. (There's nothing funnier than people like me being pompous trying to find a reason for something that may not have a reason at all.) Perhaps the instigators of the movement, chief among them the writer Hugo Ball, simply wanted a name that had no links with the world that they wished to change through their art. They wanted to overthrow the cultural values of a society that had created terrible horrors: endless parades of mutilated soldiers and the mass deaths of the First World War. Shock at humans' ability to be horrible can often give rise to a kind of crazy, desperate and absurd play. With Dada we see art, and play, as an escape from a reality that had proved itself to be brutal, ugly and joyless. But Dada wouldn't simply use art to escape the world: it was going to take the world and repurpose it in the form of Dadaism.

No surprise – the board of directors of the Society of Independent Artists objected to Duchamp's *Fountain* and excluded it from the Society's upcoming exhibition at the Grand Central Palace which opened to the public on 10 April 1917. The Board explained: 'The *Fountain* may be a very useful object in its place, but its place is not in an art exhibition and it is, by no definition, a work of art.' (Naumann 2012, p.72.) I love that comment that it 'may be a very useful object in its place'. Of course it's useful; people pee in it! The very act of having a 'definition' of art excluded any prospect of play. The inflexible Society believed the merely 'useful' could not and should not cross over into the rarefied (and usually very posh) domain of

Surrealist Doodles

Can you imagine something *more* strange than a lobster phone? A teacup with whiskers? Banana with laces? A saucepan crying? A car eating a hamburger? Surrealist works of art mix the everyday with the unusual to produce results that make you think ...

Try a surreal sketch in the space opposite.

art. But Dadaism was all about playing with where objects are, and the Dadaists had a total disregard for how things 'should' be – something we see children do from a young age, but as we grow older we tend to start seeing the world as a more fixed and structured order.

So what had Duchamp actually done?

The Board didn't appreciate the fact that Duchamp had looked at lots of different items, wondered about them and chosen the urinal above all other objects; he had played with what is or is not an 'art object'; the play of ideas about what is or is not beautiful; and its playful naming (it is, most definitely, neither a drinking fountain nor the sort of ornate fountain you might expect to see looking gorgeous in a park or courtyard). And we might wonder whether there is a playful suggestion here of the 'fountain' that goes into the urinal when men do a pee?

Within a day or so of the exhibition opening, Duchamp found the work. It had been hidden behind a partition, and he took it to be photographed by the well-known photographer and gallery owner Alfred Stieglitz. What Stieglitz wrote about *Fountain* is one of the first commentaries on this new kind of art, and Stieglitz himself plays with the form of art criticism: 'The "Urinal" photograph is really quite a wonder – Everyone who has seen it thinks it beautiful – And it's true – it is. It has an oriental look about it – a cross between a Buddha and a Veiled Woman' (Naumann 2012, p.74). There's that word again – 'wonder'. And we're back to that concept of wonder overturning reason through play – logically, we know it is a urinal, but Stieglitz has turned the image over in his mind, played with it and come up with a new species, a hybrid of Buddha and a woman wearing a veil! (Think about that for a moment. Think of a statue of Buddha slowly turning into a woman with a veil ... and back to Buddha.) Duchamp's playfulness in creating an art work has led to yet another kind of playfulness: Stieglitz's interpretation of it. We could call this the 'chain of play'. (I've just made that up.)

Fountain was Duchamp's most infamous example of an art form that he called 'ready-mades' or, to use the French phrase, 'objet trouvé', meaning literally 'found object'. This usually refers to the finding of an object – and it can be anything, stones, part of a tree, a tin can – and placing it somewhere away from its usual surroundings, so that we can look at the object differently. By seeing the object as art, rather than rubbish or clutter, we are able to appreciate a value in it that we would normally have overlooked – look at the font on that matchbox, the crystalline swirl on that stone or the depth of colour in that brick. Rather than trying to bring art into the world, we are bringing the world into art, and so redefining both 'art' and 'world'. Anyone can do it – why don't you give it a go today? Find an object – a stone, a broken-off handle, a bottle-opener – put it somewhere unexpected and then give it a title that gives it a new meaning. Or use the objects to make faces.

Of course, the presenting of *Fountain* as art didn't happen on its own. Across all the art forms poets, novelists, musicians and dancers were experimenting with creating new styles, new ideas, new feelings for the arts. These movements fed into each other – before Dadaism we had Cubism, fracturing and reassembling the everyday and laying the groundwork for Duchamp and his contemporaries. Then Dadaism in turn gave rise to Surrealism, pushing the everyday into increasingly bizarre dreamscapes. These movements subverted the art that came before, altering and playing with the way we see reality. The father of Cubism, Pablo Picasso, famously painted a woman's face from two or more angles, so that we can view her several ways within the same frame. Some people thought this was crazy but others asked, 'Isn't this how we see people anyway? Nothing stays still, we move, the person we're looking at moves, so we keep seeing each other from different angles within a split second.' So by playing with the idea that art should be purely representative, Picasso has actually given us something that is, in some ways, closer to real life. Try it: if there's someone in the room with you, look at them. Now move slightly, move back, move again. Think of the different views of that person's head you've just seen and instead of thinking of those different views being one or two seconds after each other, think of them as being at the same time. Did you do that? Then, you're a Cubist.

Picasso and Georges Braque, the other co-founder of the Cubist movement, started to experiment with reordering the world around them by cutting up existing graphic forms such as wallpaper, asking why should we stick to the established stuff that is produced by paint and brush when the world is full of ready-made things that we can pull apart, reassemble, glue together and display? The German artist Kurt Schwitters assembled bits of junk into works that are not quite painting, not quite sculpture, but a fantastical amalgam of both. The French artist Henri Matisse adapted the old 'craft' of paper-cutting to create images out of 'cut-outs' using simple coloured paper (perhaps most famously, his own representation of *The Fall of Icarus*). The German artist Hannah Höch was one of several Dadaists who developed photomontage and collage; she created bizarre creatures like the Snipplesnapplewings and Unsatisfeedle from photos of everyday objects and textures in her Magical Realm of Fantasy.'It looks, deliberately, like a children's picture book, but can it not be both an art work and an item of play? By the way, look again at those names: Snipplesnapplewings and Unsatisfeedle. They make me want to come up with some names like that and see if I can make a creature out of cut-up coloured paper to fit the names. Or perhaps the other way round: make a creature and give it a name like that.

All this suggests that the relationship between the artist, their approach to play and the world was changing. Central to the old relationship, as represented by the Romantics and others before them, was the idea of the artist who looks and observes and then, through apprenticeship, guidance and experimentation, finds ways to represent views of that world that are familiar to the art consumer. The new and playful ways of approaching art introduced by Picasso, Duchamp, Höch and many others suggested that bits of the world itself could be brought into art, by selecting them or breaking them off and placing them in the context of picture frames, galleries and photographs.

Most of this, no matter how deadly serious the artists were, required a spirit of playfulness. Yes, wallpaper is wallpaper and it goes on walls, but what if I cut it up and see what shapes and

NEWSPAPERS

Flick through newspapers or magazines and find two pictures
that are the total opposite of one another. Pin them below.

Why not try a whole collage? Make a scene. Cut out heads of famous people and put them onto the bodies of animals. Mess about with proportions: find a close-up picture of an insect and put it next to a very small picture of a person. Or go abstract and make a pattern out of fifty cut-out hands.

colours and contrasts it makes? What if I take a bicycle seat and handlebars, what can I make with that? A bull's head! Now it's not a bicycle seat and handlebars ... or is it? Can it be both: the ready-made bits of bike and the bull's head at the same time, so that we see and feel both in an instant of looking? Does that mean that when we come to see bikes after that, we'll notice bull-like things about them? Perhaps. On London Bridge Station, just at the top of one of the escalators, I saw the end of a girder sticking out of the wall. I saw above it two big bolts. They became eyes, and the end of the girder became an open mouth crying out for something. Look out, there are faces everywhere. What are they saying? What can they see? What are they thinking?

Flaming Giraffes and Melting Clocks

The Surrealists, a group officially founded in 1924 by the French writer and poet André Breton, were the direct inheritors of Dada, and they created yet another use for play. They accepted Sigmund Freud's idea that we have an 'unconscious' or 'subconscious', a space in our 'psyche' where we put our repressed thoughts. These are the thoughts and feelings that we have that we can't admit to. (I dare you to spend ten seconds thinking of a thought that you don't dare admit to to anyone else.) This kind of thought arises, Freud argues, from desires and needs and conflicts that we have when we are very young, mostly in relation to our mothers and fathers. Because we can't admit to them, we 'repress' them. That is, we put these 'conflicts' into some kind of Forgetting Room. (I've made that name up, and now I've made it up, I quite like it. I might come back to it some day and write a poem about what is in my Forgetting Room. You could have a go at that too.) Freud argued that we can find what these thoughts are through such things as dreams, slips of the tongue (now often referred to as 'Freudian slips'), déjà vu (that's the funny sensation you have when you think you've seen, heard or done something you've done before but you're not sure when or where) and analysing repetitive out-of-control activity like endless hand-washing or the repeated counting of objects.

The Surrealists thought that they could play with this, and find their way into the world of dreams through painting, sculpture and poetry. Surrealism pushed Dadaism's playfulness one step further – familiar objects don't just appear out of context but are often distorted, such as Salvador Dalí's famous melting clocks or his flaming giraffe, or Louise Bourgeois's *The Red Room*, in which everything is 'normal' in shape but everything is red.

It's not always clear, when looking at a Surrealist painting, whether the artist was creating what he or she had seen in their own dreams or whether they were trying to create something that might allow us to find some of these repressed thoughts in ourselves – or it could be both, of course. Whichever it may be, there is a strong element of play involved. Instead of saying simply, 'This is what I saw' or 'This is something I saw and this is how I saw it' or even 'This is something I saw and you can feel how I saw it through the way I've painted it', Surrealist art says, 'I'm not painting what I see or even how I saw something. I'm playing around to find out what thoughts, especially repressed and forbidden ones, are in my mind and come to the surface.'

One key way in which Surrealist painting works is by putting together elements or processes that you wouldn't expect to see together. (Try it: you could take an orange, say, and put it on the saddle of a horse. Why did I think of that? Now you try.) In the paintings of René Magritte we find someone looking in a mirror but the image in the mirror is not the 'correct' reflection; it's the back of the person's head, not the face. We can take this as some kind of joke, a kind of knowing mistake, if you like. Or we can wonder about what kind of wish or desire is represented in the painting. Is this someone who wishes that he could see the back of his head? Or that he would love it if he didn't have to see his own face when he looks in the mirror? Why would that be? Does he not like his face? Is he ashamed of his face? Does his face show something of himself that he doesn't want to see? Is it painful to look in the mirror and see something of ourselves that we are ashamed of? Would we rather 'repress' that? Fair enough, let's have a mirror that shows the back of your head instead of the front. Once you see how this kind of drawing and painting works, you can try it yourself. Why not draw some things you see which you remember from when you were very, very young and arrange them in a way that tells us how you were thinking: that a table or a cat could be huge, your hand could be tiny, a fridge could have teeth, that there was a crocodile under your bed. Do you know the book by Judith Kerr, *The Tiger Who Came to Tea?* Who is that Tiger?

Again there is a childlike element to this kind of play. Think again of Magritte's mirror – have you ever seen a child, too young to understand the concept of 'mirrors', play in front of one? It is an early part of the journey into controlling something through play – look, I can make that baby in the mirror wave its left hand, or chew its right toes. Magritte is tapping back into the early fascination with representations of the self that is one of the very earliest forms of childhood play.

Salvador Dalí created an old-school type of telephone where the receiver is a lobster. Two 'real' things are brought together here in an unlikely or impossible juxtaposition. At one level it is once again that age-old 'what if' game: what if the receiver were ... a lobster? Imagine lifting that up by mistake in the dark! Eurghhh! The piece invites us to play these kinds of mind games. But we might also ask what drives someone to think of the phone as a lobster. Is there an underlying fear that the phone contains something unknown, a conversation, an interaction, that you cannot predict? Something that lurks out of sight deep down, submerged, and might snap at you? What kind of unpleasant things will I hear if I lift it up? Lobstery words? Can you say or write the words that might be coming out of the lobster? Why is someone speaking to us through a lobster? Am I afraid of what I might hear if I think of the receiver as a sharp, hard, bitey, nippy thing? Are you?

Surrealist paintings, sculptures and assemblages are full of images like these. At one level they can be taken almost as jokes or strange comments. At another, they can ask us to play around with the kinds of thoughts that perhaps we have 'repressed', and through play we can safely access and explore these thoughts that we would otherwise avoid out of fear.

Deface your Darlings

Duchamp didn't just take the everyday and turn it into art – he dared to take existing art and play with it too. For his piece *L.H.O.O.Q.*, he took a reproduction of da Vinci's famous painting *Mona Lisa* and pencilled in a moustache.

Print out a famous work of art – painting, photograph or sculpture – no piece, no matter how revered, is safe – and make it your own! Maybe that girl should actually have a *pear* ear-ring? *Starry Night* is missing a spaceship? Does that self-portrait by Van Gogh need a pair of sunglasses?

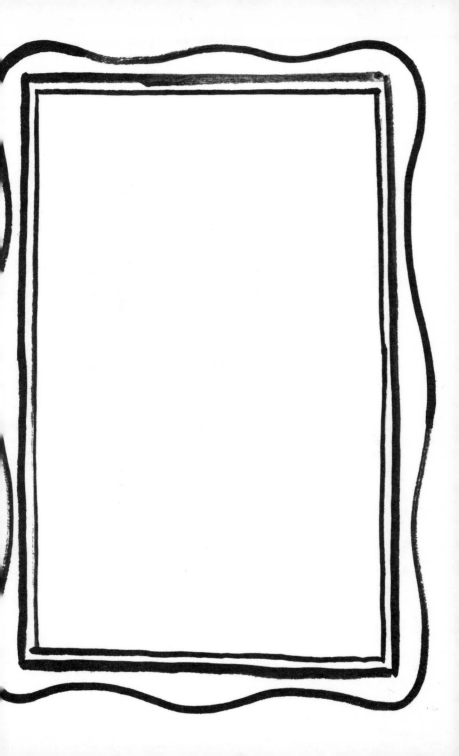

The End

We began with a far distant ancestor, playing with an old vulture bone and a mammoth tusk, beginning a process of experimentation and first sparking that sense of 'wonder' that allowed us to develop, artistically, socially, individually. Through making art (painting, sculpture, collages, design) we humans have taught ourselves to play with the visual. And without that, we would never have been able to come up with a phone that looks like a lobster. The history of art is also the history of play, which is also the history of us. Oh I like that: the history of play is the history of us. There's another one of those 'aphorisms' I'm fond of. Aphphphphph ... or ... ism!

As we have changed, our art has changed, and how we have defined art has changed, but that fundamental instinct to play, experiment, repurpose, test and reimagine has always been central. Just as play is a deliberate pushing of the boundaries, so art has refused to be solely defined by one idea or one set of people.

Playfulness in art has allowed us to see the world anew by framing the objects, items and ideas around us in different ways, inviting us to play with the ideas and feelings that we see, or imagine that we can see, in the art. We do this by playing with ideas and feelings that existed in our own heads before we looked at the piece of art in the first place. Looking at art work becomes a creative form of play in itself.

So you could give this a go: you can change how you see the world today. You can make time today to go out and play – or, if you prefer, let's say 'make some art'. After all, as we've discussed, the two really are very similar. Or perhaps you would prefer to go and look at some art (and remember, art can be found where you least expect it – such as London Bridge Station, on the wall at the top of the escalator), and think about it – playfully.

Or, as I once put it in a poem called 'Colour':

Take a brush:
The sky is green
The grass is blue
You are purple
The house is silver
The sun is black
The river is gold
The world has changed
Did you do that?

Aesthetics

Think a red thought

~~~~~~~

Think a blue thought

Think a green thought

Think a yellow thought

Think a purple thought

Think an orange thought

Think a clear
transparent thought

WORD PLAY

Language is the main way – though not the only way – we convey and think of ideas. When we play with words, we play with ideas. Try this: 'In this raspberry I want to look at playing with words.' All I've done is paraphrase the first sentence in this paragraph and introduce one new word. Suddenly, I've conjured up the idea that you and me are looking inside a raspberry. Now, you have a go. Take away 'raspberry' and put another word in its place. What does it make you think of?

The more we play with words, the more we play with ideas, and in this raspberry – sorry, I mean chapter – I'll look at a bit of history of wordplay and the history of wordplay in ourselves, starting with when we are very young.

Child's Play

When my stepdaughter Laura was three, she would sometimes stand in the middle of the kitchen, spread her arms wide as if she was the star in a musical and burst into song. Her songs were not written, composed songs. They were improvised show-stoppers, belted out to an imagined theatre full of adoring fans. I wrote one of them down, as she sang it:

Happy-happy,
happy birthday cake,
happy birthday cake.
The cake,
the cake,
the cake,
the door,
and the door.
And the door is open.
Merry merry Mary.
Merry Mary merry.
Merry, merry.
Da dee-dee.
Dubba dee-dee.

Naomi go to school.
Yes.
Oh yes.
My pyjamas go to school.
Pyjamas go to school.
Merry merry Mary.
The dolly is on the water.
The book is on the water.
The paper is on the water.
On the water,
the water,
on the water.

I went on the phone.
I called the phone.
I went in the tar-tar.
I went in the boo-boo.
I went in another boo.
Shop-shopping.
Shop-shopping.
Shop-shopping.
I make a pizza.
The pizza.
Mucky pizza.
Mucky pizza.
Pizza in the bathroom.
I eat the bathroom
I eat the door.
I eat the bath ...

... I tired now.

I not sing any more.

Such outbursts of improvised language and music can happen very quickly, and there may only be a very small window in a person's life when we feel free enough to produce such a thing. I think they remind us of what our minds and bodies can do when we are this free – just as freestyle poets and ad-lib artists across all the arts know only too well. They are outbursts, flowerings of freely associated words, thoughts and ideas.

Limerick

A limerick is a five-line poem that's often funny – and sometimes rude. It generally follows the rhyme scheme AABBA, so the first two lines and the last line rhyme with each other, and the third and the fourth lines rhyme with each other. Limericks usually open with a person and where they're from:

THERE WAS A YOUNG LADY FROM TWICKENHAM.

WHOSE BOOTS WERE TOO TIGHT TO WALK QUICK IN 'EM

WHEN SHE CAME IN FROM HER WALK

SHE WAS WHITER THAN CHALK;

SO SHE TOOK OFF HER BOOTS AND WAS SICK IN 'EM.

Your turn! Find a map, close your eyes and point to a location. That's where the subject of your limerick is from – it'll be the last word in the first line of your poem.

Without wanting to put a dampener on the spontaneous, exuberant brilliance of Laura's song, it's worth taking a few moments to look at what she is doing here.

She picks a word or phrase up from conversations she's heard and plays with it, just as we might play with anything you can reshape, like Play-Doh or sand – language is, in many ways, simply another material that we can manipulate through play. The way she does this involves several different methods:

- taking a word or phrase and repeating it so that it makes a rhythm – as with 'shop-shopping' and 'mucky pizza';

- taking a phrase and repeating the same shape (technically, the same 'syntax'), while changing a word in that phrase, as with 'I went in the tar-tar, I went in the boo-boo';

- making up or using nonsense words, as with 'da dee-dee', 'boo-boo';

- playing with the sounds inside words, as with 'merry merry Mary, merry Mary merry';

- using 'free association' between words as a trigger for creating the next moment, as with 'book' and 'paper', 'phone' and 'tar-tar' (goodbye), 'pizza' and 'eat'.

Perhaps you can see other methods at work too. You can jot them down in the margin of this page.

Why would a three-year-old do this? My view is that this is a fascinating moment in a child's mental, physical and linguistic development. She has grasped the basic grammar of her mother tongue: for example, she can use verbs to vary between past and present (like 'I eat' and 'I went'); she can name and talk about a wide range of the objects and processes in her life; but – this is the important bit – the grammar and language of the everyday are sufficiently new to her for her to be still curious enough about them to want to play with them. And she's doing this in order to see and feel the potential in language, and to explore what language can do for her. Ah, if only we could all think like this! If only all of us could think of language as something that has 'potential', rather than as something that we just have to obey! Laura experiments with the sound of language ('phonology'), its meaning ('semantics') and its grammar; she experiments with how, in English, we can add on or take bits off words ('morphology'), as she does with 'shop-shopping'. When we speak and write, we operate on all these levels at the same time, mostly on a subconscious level without even thinking about it.

Laura is at precisely the moment where the phonology of language is still very intense – this begins before we are born – but, whereas a few months earlier she couldn't easily voice the words for the objects and processes around her, now she can. She can pour all these new words and phrases into her fascination with sound. That's another way of putting it: Laura is playing with sound – but not any old sound she has come across. It's the sound that she is discovering that she can make with her lungs, throat, tongue, teeth and mouth. The making and hearing of sound are a physical thing, and

WORD LADDER

Turn one word into another by changing one letter and only using real words: can you get from SEAM to MEAT? Or from RIME to GURN?

SCORE
SNORE
STORE
SHORE

SEAM

_____

_____

_____

MEAT

she is discovering variations and potentials in what and how she can make it. In a few months' time the power of naming and grammatical mastery will expand while the fascination with the sound of the language will diminish. Note, I didn't say 'disappear' – just 'diminish'. So she's at a moment at we might call 'peak wordplay'. Can we as older children or adults re-find that fascination with the sound of words? Can we re-find the fun we have when we change the sound and discover a new meaning pops out. Or a new moaning. Or a new morning. Or a new mooning.

While Laura's focus may be on the sounds she is making, when we play with sounds, we nearly always end up playing with meaning anyway! How come? Because no matter how nonsensical, and seemingly neglectful, we are of making sense, words still end up giving us meanings anyway. If I say 'chair', I suspect that you will think of these four-legged things we sit on in our homes and places of work. I'm sitting on one as I'm writing this. What colour do you think it is? And when we repeat words and phrases we create an unstated meaning. If I say, 'Rain, rain, rain, rain', you may well guess that I mean it's been raining a lot. But I didn't say that. I just repeated the word 'rain'! Laura sang, 'On the water, the water, on the water'. Perhaps it has a hidden meaning or sense that comes through repetition: emphasis and praise. Repetition touches our senses in playful ways for the person saying it or the person hearing it. (By the way, the chair I'm sitting on is white. Well, it was white, but it's gone a bit grey.)

I will confess here that over the years I have stolen three-year-old Laura's way of thinking and speaking, and when I write poems for children, there are times when I've imitated something of her wordplay. At the back of my mind, I've thought, if this is how two- and three-year-olds teach themselves speech and language, I could write poems that could reach children who, perhaps, don't play with words in this way. And, if you don't play with words, then you don't discover the potential of language and you might not discover your own potential to use language and to communicate. And that would be sad.

Here's me owing something to Laura's wordplay:

Top button
Bottom button
Top button
Top.

Bottom button
Top button
Bottom button
Bop.

Bop .... bop
Bottom button top.
Bop .... bop
Bottom button bop.

By playing with the sounds of words that have some echoing similarity with each other – 'bottom', 'button', 'top' and 'bop' – and by muddling them up, I imply a meaning: that when we're doing our buttons up we can get muddled and put the wrong

Metaphysics

If you had to describe yourself using only five words, what would they be?

button in the button-hole. It's 'nonsense', but it's not-nonsense too. Can I call it new-sense instead of nonsense? Thanks.

Now, we could leave Laura in her glorious three-year-old bubble and me in my wish to play in a similar vein and say to ourselves, 'How delightful'. By describing it as a particular moment in her development (and, ahem ahem, mine!), I am also consigning it to immaturity, infant behaviour, 'childishness' even. Turn that on its head, and it doesn't take long to realise that the play that Laura is into here is not far from the word- and sound-play that serious songwriters, speech-writers, playwrights, scriptwriters and poets go in for too. And we all do similar things in everyday speech. Listen carefully to how we retell a story many times: we settle on rhythms and rhythmic patterns. In the 1980s a ninety-six-year-old neighbour used to tell me what happened when a bomb fell at the other end of her street: 'All the knockers on the doors went rap-rap-rap-rap-rap down Pedro Street.' She told me this in exactly the same way, many, many times. When people describe a journey they do very often, or a repeated action they do at work, they often create a rhythmic way of talking about it. An ex-miner once told me:

> I go to work,
> to earn money,
> to buy bread,
> to build up my strength
> to go to work,
> to earn money,
> to buy bread,
> to build up my strength,
> to go to work ...

What's going on here is that through repetition wordplay and sound-play, people are able to make something of a joke – perhaps a bitter one – about their repetitive daily grind. The point is made through wordplay! And the point is made through the game of making the chant endless.

Witty Words

It's hard to pin the word 'wit' down to a specific meaning. Wit often involves playing with our expectations and playing with meaning, putting words alongside each other in ways that echo each other in unexpected and fun or funny ways. We seem to like that use of language.

We can see wit at work in some of the earliest recorded examples of English that we have. The language that settlers from the European continent brought to what we now call the British Isles was the language of the Germanic tribes such as the Angles, Saxons, Jutes, Frisians and Franks. Some people call this language 'Anglo-Saxon', but linguists prefer to call it 'Old English'.

Some time around the year 970, a scribe wrote down some riddles. Riddles are a way of talking about the things and ideas we live with in mysterious and intriguing ways. Often we 'set' a riddle and ask someone to 'get' it. It's not only a playful way of handling things in our lives, but it is a game in itself. We don't know why this person back in 970 did such a thing other

Encyclopedia

One player decides on a topic (it could be names of countries, footballers, actors). Taking turns, go through the alphabet and come up with a word for each letter.

Two people playing might say:

Australia

Burundi

Cambodia

Denmark

And so on...

than to state the obvious: the people who wrote, read, spoke and heard these riddles thought they were intriguing, witty and stimulating.

Let's go back to 970, then, and play. Here, using the alphabet of the time are the first three words of one of the riddles:

Moððe word fræt

It means, 'A moth ate words'. A little later the riddle says, something like: 'Though the thieving stranger swallowed the word, he was not one jot the wiser.'

What is the answer to this riddle? Who is the moth, and who is the thieving stranger?

(I'll give you a clue: a moth at one point in its life cycle is a caterpillar or larva.)

The answer is: a bookworm. It eats words but is none the wiser for it. (Perhaps with all that explanation from me, the gag is lost. Sorry!)

And riddles are still going strong. Over a thousand years later, when I visit schools, children come up to me and try their riddles out on me. What goes round the world but stays in the corner? What gets wetter the more it dries? What is it, the more you have, the less you see? (Can you answer these?) As with the Old English riddle, this kind of play with words is 'paradox': a postage stamp goes round the world but stays in the corner of the envelope; a towel gets wetter as it dries you;

the more darkness you have, the less able you are to see. See if you can work some paradoxes into a riddle: think of a clock ... it has a face but no head. A chair has legs but can't walk. You can't put a knife and fork on the kind of table that's a timetable.

Staying with the Anglo-Saxons for a moment, they and the Vikings seem to have embedded some of this riddling mindset into a lot of their poetry, with the use of what are called 'kennings'. Rather than talk directly of the sea, Old English poets might call it a 'whale-road', blood could be 'battle-sweat' and the sun a 'heaven-candle'. We haven't lost this way of thinking: think of compound words like 'ankle-biter' and 'rugrat' to describe very small children, or indeed 'bookworm' again to describe someone who loves reading. Or how about scene-stealer, show-stopper, page-turner and cliff-hanger? Can you make up some new ones and get other people to guess what you're talking about?

Puns and Nonsense

Puns are ways of finding two meanings in the same sounds of two different words. What are the strongest shellfish? Mussels.

Puns have been around for a long time. In Geoffrey Chaucer's masterpiece *The Canterbury Tales* you can find, say, a pun on the words we now write as 'farthing' (the coin) and 'farting', which were at the time pronounced in exactly the same way. This is another aspect of punning, where we surprise people

 ansom Note Poetry

Dig out old newspapers and magazines – the more different the subjects, the better – and cut out loads of both familiar and unusual words. Move the words around on a piece of paper and turn them into a poem. Will you be able to make it rhyme? Or at least make sense? Then again – does it need to do either?

who might be expecting something ordinary and we get something rude instead.

Sometimes a pun will stretch the meaning of the words so far that it becomes nonsense. The word 'nonsense' sounds as if it means 'no sense'. In fact, all nonsense has some sense and, as I suggested earlier, it quite often it has a lot of new sense. In Shakespeare's *King Lear* there is a good bit of nonsense spoken by the Fool, and another character called Edgar who disguises himself as 'Poor Tom', and even Lear himself, who seems to become mentally ill, or 'mad' in old parlance.

Here is Edgar, disguised as Poor Tom, explaining why and how everything has gone wrong in his life – supposedly. The 'foul fiend' is the devil. The picture that Poor Tom conjures up is of the devil leading him through fire, rivers and bogs, playing terrible tricks on him. Then, when he gets to the end of it, Poor Tom starts making funny noises and calling out for help. If you can, please, please, please read this out loud in a desperate, crazy voice. Maybe, do it in a pair, like a singing duet. Play with it! Beat out a rhythm on a table or a chair or with your feet on the floor. Pull on your hair. Pull at your face.

> Who gives any thing to poor Tom? whom the foul
> fiend hath led through fire and through flame, and
> through ford and whirlipool e'er bog and quagmire;
> that hath laid knives under his pillow, and halters
> in his pew; set ratsbane by his porridge; made him
> proud of heart, to ride on a bay trotting-horse over
> four-inched bridges, to course his own shadow for a

traitor. Bless thy five wits! Tom's a-cold, – O, do
de, do de, do de. Bless thee from whirlwinds,
star-blasting, and taking! Do poor Tom some
charity, whom the foul fiend vexes: there could I
have him now, – and there, – and there again, and there.

This speech moves towards nonsense as it piles one torment on top of another in a great rush of torments. This babbling has been one of the techniques of nonsense. It's almost as if by creating a rush of words, the usual method of language to communicate and refer to things is pushed aside by the massive overproduction of images.

Of course it's not only the great Shakespeare who was brilliant at nonsense. We all are. For many years, perhaps going back to Shakespeare's time, children have recited versions of this seemingly nonsensical recitation:

Ladles and jellyspoons,
I come before you to stand behind you
and tell you something I know nothing about.
Next Friday, the day before Thursday,
there will be a ladies' meeting
for men only. Wear your best clothes, if you haven't any, and if
you can come,
please stay home.
Admission is free,
you can pay at the door.
We'll give you a seat,
so you can sit on the floor.

It doesn't matter where you sit,
the man in the gallery
is sure to spit.

Another early form of nonsense poetry was the limerick:

There was an Old Woman named Towl
Who went out to Sea with her Owl,
 But the Owl was Sea-sick
 And scream'd for Physic;
Which sadly annoy'd Mistress Towl.

Now that we've perfected the limerick form, this doesn't seem too great, but it has at its heart the ingredients that millions since have taken to create their own satirical, nonsensical, random portraits of people and places. In a jaunty rhythm, which speeds up in the middle, the people of limericks are made fallible, malleable and often destructible – frequently never to recover. In the action there is often some impossible or odd occurrence, as with this lady going to sea with an owl: why? how? Ideally, there should be no reason given! Ideally, some kind of upset should occur, leaving the main figure disrupted, dissolved or even eliminated. This tradition is the very opposite of the restorative, redemptive literature where things all work out well, or at least, improved, in the end – as in most children's books.

These nonsense poems play with our need for order, which most of us spend a good deal of time, effort and money trying to create. The limerick form seems to be particularly satisfying to our ear because it appears to be very ordered:

an opening couplet which sets out the scene, two quick lines which describe the havoc, and a last line which is really a kind of hoax: rhythmically it 'resolves' the poem rather as music in the major key resolves back to the 'tonic' or 'doh' note. But where havoc has been created, the last line may well confirm it or even add to it. Modern limericks may well save the total disaster for the last line, usually ending with a new rhyming word. To write a limerick is to play a game with rules. In a way it's a challenge to beat the game: can you stick to this form and surprise and amaze us with a yet more daft, disruptive bit of mayhem, held in check by the exact meter and rhyme scheme?

The master of the nonsense poem was Edward Lear. Lear began writing his limericks to entertain some children he met when he was hired to paint an aristocrat's menagerie. One of the first he wrote goes:

> There was an Old Man with a beard,
> Who said, 'It is just as I feared!
> Two Owls and a Hen,
> Four Larks and a Wren,
> Have all built their nests in my beard!'

Lear went on to write more than 200 limericks, establishing the form as one of our most popular ways of playing with words in poetry. In fact, so established has it become that there are wags aplenty who find ways to play with the limerick itself:

> There was a young man from Japan
> Whose limericks never would scan.
> When they asked him why,

Alliteration Accumulation

Alliteration is when you repeat the same initial sounds in a group of words. Like,

PETER PIPER PICKED A PECK OF PICKLED PEPPERS

Now, pick a letter and come up with the longest sentence you can in which very nearly every word starts with that same sound. The only rule is that your sentence must make sense.

A

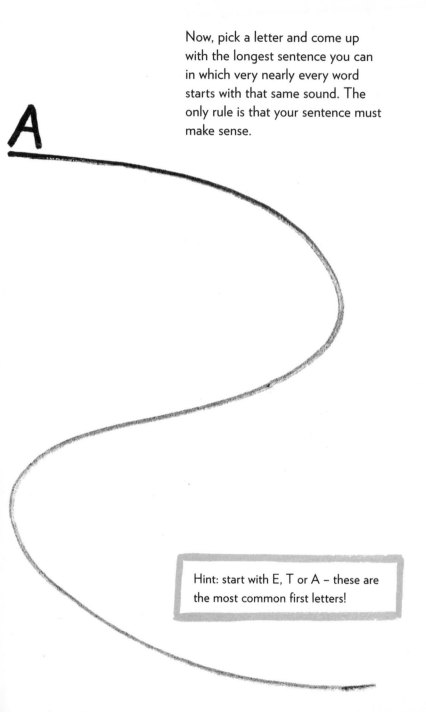

Hint: start with E, T or A – these are the most common first letters!

He said, with a sigh,
'It's because I always try to get as many words into the last line
as I possibly can.'

There are thousands more which are unrepeatable here,
reminding us that one way in which people treat taboo and
'rude' subjects is to take the words we use to describe those
taboos and line them up in a nicely ordered way. There is a
playful contrast between the disruption caused by mentioning
taboo subjects and the order and control of the limerick form.

But Lear was more than a limerick writer: he invented a strange,
eerie, surreal narrative poetry in which unreal or unlikely
creatures make odd or pointless journeys. The most famous of
these has to be 'The Owl and the Pussycat', which has become
so familiar that it's easy to forget its oddness. Owls don't marry
cats, owls marry owls and cats marry cats (we might say!); you
don't get wedding rings from pigs' noses (and even if you could,
you might have second thoughts about getting one that way).
And is a turkey licensed to conduct a marriage? As if to remind
us of the impossibility of this romance and marriage, Lear used
one of his invented words:

They dined on mince and slices of quince,
which they ate with a runcible spoon

What is a 'runcible spoon'? What are you picturing right now,
as an owl and a cat eat with a runcible spoon? How do we
picture something when all we are given is a nonsense image
and a made-up word? Usually we pull in words that sound like
the nonsense word, so that we can explain what it means. I

can hear words like 'rinse' and 'once' and 'fancy' and 'trance', telling me that maybe this spoon is magical in some way. You could right now make up another word to describe a spoon. A plungerish spoon? That would be the kind of spoon that plunges into porridge very easily.

Hiding behind this poem, are there worries about being odd or different and longing to be away somewhere with no one else but a loved one? Have such thoughts and feelings been hidden in the play of nonsense verse? Does wordplay help poets conceal their fears, anxieties and desires? We know from biographies that Lear was afraid that he wasn't like the people around him. Was he expressing that fear in this simple nonsense poem? You see, when we investigate play, we can sometimes surprise ourselves with what we find.

In my favourite Lear poem, 'The Jumblies', some creatures sail away (there's that repeated motif of going away again!) in a sieve. Right away we know that the poem is a kind of play session, a journey full of play: of course, you can't sail on water in a sieve, but even so the Jumblies manage it. They get somewhere, and then ... they come back. It's a long and hazardous journey but with no point to it. And perhaps that is the point! The point in some of our journeys is really to be found in the journey itself and not in the place you get to. The problem with getting somewhere is that you end up where you started: with yourself. The great thing about journeys – going or coming back – is that you have to manage the journey, you're in transit, you're on the way, unsettled, not attached, neither here nor there, going through the portal, experiencing change. Through the play with nonsense ideas, nonsense language and

Exquisite Corpse

Here's a sentence:

BEAUTIFUL ROSES MELT IN A PURPLE COAT

In a group, take it in turns replacing each word with another word like it. So you replace an adjective for another adjective, a verb for another verb, a noun for another noun and so on. (You're allowed to use 'the' and 'a' and 'an' as you want.

Some others to start:

AN ILLUSTRATED WOMAN RUNS TOWARDS YELLOW FIELDS

Or:

THE DARK BLUE SONG ENTERS BESIDE A RED BOTTLE

Meaningless or deeply moving? Surprise each other with impossible word pictures.

nonsense creatures, Edward Lear creates a journey that is like all journeys perhaps – or even the journey of life itself? – without ever telling us that this is what he's doing. He's hidden these big questions behind the play of nonsense. Why not daydream a nonsense journey? How are you travelling? Who do you go with? Where do you get to? Who or what do you meet? What do you see? What's the weather like? Do you come back? If you do, what do people say?

Borogoves and Mome Raths

No one has done more to turn wordplay into a philosophical debate about what words can or can't do than Lewis Carroll. (His real name was Charles Lutwidge Dodgson – he took Charles, made it into Latin 'Carolus' and turned that into Carroll. He took Lutwidge, found the English version and created Lewis Carroll. I could pretend to be a female author and call myself Rose Michaelson! See what you could do with your name to create a pseudonym.) The two Alice books are forever probing whether words do the job we all say they do: which is to communicate meaning. Do words really mean what we think they mean? If they don't, is the world really what we say that it is? To explore this, Carroll sent Alice off to another world. In this strange place she is the voice of reason and everyone else is absurd, illogical or a disrupter of all that Alice knows or thinks is true. As with Lear's runcible spoon, we witness the creation of new words which don't appear at first to have meaning, but which, as none other than Humpty Dumpty himself explains, do contain meaning ... or do they? After all, why should be believe what a talking egg says?

Alice asks Humpty Dumpty to explain the poem 'Jabberwocky'. Below is the first verse of the poem:

'Twas brillig, and the slithy toves
Did gyre and gimble in the wabe;
All mimsy were the borogoves,
And the mome raths outgrabe.

Humpty Dumpty gives Alice the meanings for the words she doesn't know – which is most of them. For example, as Humpty explains to Alice:

BRILLIG: 'Brillig' means four o'clock in the afternoon – the time when you begin broiling things for dinner.

TOVES: 'toves' are something like badgers – they're something like lizards – and they're something like corkscrews ... also they make their nests under sun-dials – also they live on cheese.

OUTGRABE: 'outgribing' is something between bellowing and whistling, with a kind of sneeze in the middle.

Did the poet make up the words? Is Humpty Dumpty making up the meanings? Perhaps the poet and the egg character are working at cross-purposes, and so the poem becomes something quite different for the two of them. What do you think 'brillig' means? What do you think a 'mome rath' is? You don't have to take Humpty's word for it. After all, he's going to fall off that wall in a bit and not even all the king's horses and all the king's men are going to put him back together again. Hang on – how in heaven's name would a king's horse be able to put an egg back together again?

The Alice books are dangerous. They lead us down paths where we are sometimes left wondering things like, if we don't really know what words mean, then what do we know? After all, we go about our lives assuming that we are all agreed about the words we use. A dog is a dog is a dog. A cat is a cat is a cat. Sorted. If you put me in a world where people are using English words or words that sound like English and I don't know what they mean, it feels as if I'm ignorant or stupid. The outburst of wordplay in 'Jabberwocky' is of course fantastic fun, but it's also troubling: can we really break out of the world contained in a dictionary? Can we make up words that have bits of other words in them, and tell stories, make up poems and end up telling some kind of truth? Really?

Have a go at doing this: take parts of two words and put them together to make a new word, like the first half of 'hopeful' and the second half of 'celebrity' – you get 'hopebrity' – someone who hopes that they'll be a celebrity. Or how about slushy mud? Slud. I fell into some slud and I can't get my trousers clean.

Or you could take place-names and think up what they could mean, just as Douglas Adams and John Lloyd did in *The Meaning of Liff*. I was brought up in Pinner. Perhaps that's a really annoying person who comes round and pins badges on people. How about Finchley? You can feel a bit Finchley, and it means you feel a bit like a bird.

In the Alice books, the subversive idea that you can break up, disrupt and remake words is made even more dangerous because the books set up people who speak and act with great authority, people who do absurd things but who, ultimately, can all be swept aside by Alice.

The End

When you listen out for it, you can hear people playing with words and language in ads, in jokes, in everyday chat – everywhere! People have been doing it for centuries in many kinds of writing – plays, poems, stories. Doing this moves our language on, changes the way we try to make ourselves understood, helps us describe new things. Think of the hundreds of new words that people have made up to describe the digital world: internet, web page, web site, texting, email, app, key in, log out. People had to play with words to come up with these. Every time you have a go at it yourself, you become part of the great rolling stone of invention. (Ooo, there's another phrase I've made up: 'the great rolling stone of invention'.)

And remember: words are not as they appear in dictionaries, alone, one by one, under each other, in lists, with the only

Making Sense of Nonsense

Lewis Carroll's poem 'Jabberwocky' is full of nonsense words
– like 'slithy' and 'brillig'. That is, until Humpty Dumpty
explains the logic behind them. *Of course* 'slithy' means
lithe and slimy, and 'brillig' is the time you start broiling
your dinner.

Try making up words that sound like the thing they stand for:
what would you call the noise a knife makes on a plate? What
word could you make up to describe straightening something?
How about that moment where you remember that you've
forgotten something but you don't know what it is? Create
your own nonsense words. that you make out of real words,
like when smoke and fog become 'smog'. In a group, write
down the words and meanings on separate pieces of paper.
Whoever can correctly pair up the most wins!

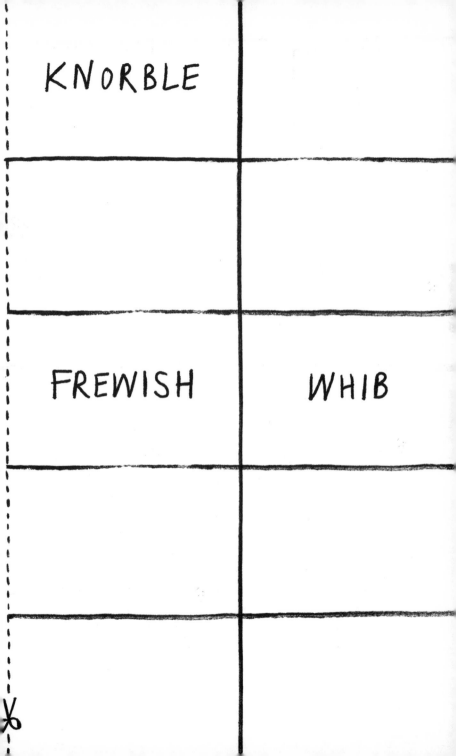

KNORBLE

FREWISH   WHIB

connection between them the alphabetical order of their first letters. Words in speech and writing are in constant, moving connection with each other. When we play with them in the countless ways at our disposal – I've only touched on a handful in this chapter – we reveal a way in which the word we are playing with hooks up with other words in phrases, sentences, speeches, passages of writing. Behind every word, then, there is another word that it sounds like, or another word we might be reminded of or another word that we might think of. Someone once called that an 'endless chain'.

Making it Up

I am an improviser, an ad-libber, a chancer and a blagger. So are you. We are all ready to give things a go, make things up on the fly – if we weren't, the human race wouldn't have survived. We might make plans – whether it's a meal, an exam, a holiday or just getting out of bed – but no matter how much we have prepared, there is always something that turns up that doesn't fit the script. Sometimes our preparation might come in handy – but sometimes it's the opposite: our plans can trip us up. We're so well prepared for one eventuality that we can't react quickly enough when things change. Ever heard the expression 'think on your feet'? Well that's what we're talking about here. Thinking when we're sitting down – reading, planning and writing – is very important, but now we're going to look at what happens when we try to think on the move.

Thinking on your feet is a kind of ad-libbing, using your wits, reacting to what's changing. The best people at thinking on their feet are the ones who have got a tool kit at the tips of their fingers, on the tip of their tongue, in the soles of their shoes, in the whites of their eyes. Let's see if we can put this tool kit together.

I was once in a car heading north on the motorway. I was the passenger. Suddenly, we were 'in a situation'. A car pulled across from one lane to another, a lorry in front of us slammed on the brakes. We were going to crash – there was no way to avoid it. My friend Ian was driving – he swerved the car past the lorry, then swerved back to avoid hitting another car that had suddenly loomed up. In a split second we had gone from being 100 per cent about to crash to rolling along with a clear road ahead of us. We carried on.

I was amazed. I was as certain as could be that I would not have been able to do that. It seemed almost magical that he had known how to do that fancy double swerve manoeuvre. Now, if Ian was a racing driver or a professional man of the road, I might not have been so impressed. But he's nothing like that. He's a magician! Really! I'm not making that up. He's a professional conjuror. I couldn't help wondering whether there was anything in the fact that he's a conjuror that helped him react so quickly and effectively.

The Writing on the Wall

I've often seen Ian's act – in fact, we've done shows together – and I know that he prepares everything perfectly. But I also know that he's brilliant at ad-libbing whenever he's faced with a heckler shouting out wisecracks and jokes. Before he goes on stage, his face sometimes looks like a lively dog – he glances about, eyebrows up, as if he's just about to say something.

He's noticing everything, and he's reacting to it. I was once backstage with him, just about to 'go on', and there was a sign that said, 'If you see anyone acting suspiciously, report it to the management.' He pointed at it and whispered to me, 'Isn't that the point though? It's a theatre. What if it's a whodunnit? Aren't people supposed to act suspiciously?'

I love this: seeing something in our surroundings, like a pretty boring sign that most of us would ignore, and improvising a joke, coming up with a reaction that makes you see what's in front of you in a new way.

Let's have a look at some great examples I've come across of people looking at ordinary everyday signage in quirky ways:

Once, when my mum and dad took me to the zoo, they told me that the sign that said 'These animals are dangerous' was pronounced, 'These animals are dangaroos', a word that rhymes with kangaroos. (Come to think of it, what is a 'dangaroo'? What does it look like? A kangaroo with fangs and boxing gloves? A giant hornet? Your turn.)

You may have seen that the lettering for 'Caffè Nero' is that square, capital letter style so that the 'o' looks a bit like a 'd'. Result? I drive my children nuts by always calling it 'Caffè Nerd'. (What do they sell in Caffè Nerd?)

I once wrote a poem about a man who got out of his car, walked up to the sign that said 'SLOW' that was painted on the surface of the road and stood there shouting, 'I'm not! I'm not!'

What would happen if...

Players take it in turns to come up with a 'what if ...' situation, and the others say what they think would happen.

What would happen if ...

- All the trees in the world had no leaves?
- All the cars were gone?
- Everybody wore the same clothes?
- You could fly?
- No one cleaned the house?
- There were no MPs?
- There were no police?
- People couldn't make babies anymore?

The poet Roger McGough told me that he had once seen a sign outside a restaurant that listed 'Today's Special', and written underneath it: 'So's every day.'

There used to be warning signs all over France that said, 'Alcohol kills slowly'. Someone had added, 'We're not in a hurry.'

Someone once saw a sign that said:

> Private
> No swimming allowed.

They noticed that you could make it say the opposite by changing the punctuation:

> Private?
> No!
> Swimming allowed.

As you can see, playing with the words and instructions around us is easy. There's a sign on a metal cover in the pavement that says CATV. I keep reading it as CAT TV. Is that the channel that cats watch when we're out the house? What do they show on CAT TV?

That's all you have to do: grab the letters, words, signs, ads, shop names around you and play. Change the punctuation, add a letter, take a letter away, pronounce it differently, pretend to misunderstand it ...

This way of thinking will help you think on your feet. It's part of the quick-witted tool box you've got at the ready.

Why don't you look around you now? Perhaps you're on a bus or train, or reading in the park, or sitting in your living room. Pick something in your eyeline – it could be a road sign, a menu, the title of a book or magazine, some graffiti, anything with words. Now, play around with it: swap one of the words, change the punctuation, make it a question (how would you answer it?), see if any of the words have other meanings. And if you find an ad lib that works, that makes you chuckle or see something in an interesting and different way, store it up for another day – add it to that mental tool box of improvisation. Comedians and performers of all kinds do this all the time: we say something or do something that seems to just pop into our head, we see that it 'works' and then we tuck it away in the back of our minds to use another time. The more you have in your mental tool box, the easier 'thinking on your feet' becomes.

A Tall Story

One of ways we ad-lib in our day-to-day life is in the way we tell the stories of things that happen to us. Ad-libbing inside these stories to shape them so that they are more dramatic or funnier or more bizarre, adding in bits to exaggerate or accentuate them, pruning out the boring bits. You could call it cheating or fibbing – or you could call it 'artistic licence'!

As a child I used to watch and listen to my dad telling a story, and see how an event that I remembered clearly started to change as he dressed up what had really happened. One time we were on holiday in Yorkshire and my brother had to leave early, to go to our home in London before heading off to France. We said goodbye to him at the station, and off he went on the train. But just a few moments later Mum realised that he hadn't taken his key to get into our house. How would he get the stuff he needed for his trip to France? Oh no! Passport! Francs (this was before the Euro)! Panic! What to do? This was long before the days of mobile phones. My Dad looked at his watch and said that he thought he could drive fast enough over the moors to catch the train at the next station. Off we went – hurtling down the winding roads, across the North Yorkshire moors, tumbling onto the station platform, where the train was already waiting. My dad rushed along the platform, looking in all the carriages. He found my brother and handed him the key. As it happens, my brother didn't seem too fussed and muttered something about how he would have found a way round it.

I watched my Dad tell this story again and again, and each time it changed a little. Now, we were taking hairpin bends at 60 m.p.h. on the manic drive against the clock, a flustered flock of sheep blocking the road parted to make way for us like Moses and the Red Sea; at one tense moment I caught sight of the train puffing through the valley below and shouted out, 'There it is! We're not going to make it!' And my favourite embellishment of all: how, when we got to the station, he had (he said!) run along the platform, waving his hands in the air, shouting 'Stop the train! Stop the train!' (He hadn't!) And then came the pay-off at the end: he acted out my brother taking the key off my father very coolly and saying in a dull, flat voice, 'I wasn't bothered, I was going to borrow a ladder from Mr Townsend' – so the whole death-defying drive had been pointless anyway!

Half the story was lies! He shaped the story into dramatic phases and scenes: would we or wouldn't we make it? The clichéd cinematic 'Stop the train!' The whole blithering anti-climax of my brother not being bothered anyway. I could see how my dad worked the events into the classic form of a story or a film. He hadn't written it down. He did it through ad-libbing it each time he told the story, seeing how friends and relatives reacted to it, finding what moments built up the tension, which moments released it as laughs.

#Titles

There's a popular ad lib game on Twitter that I particularly enjoy called #titles. We pick a theme and come up with altered titles for books, films, songs and plays based on that theme. So, for example, if the theme was #BigTitles, you have to turn a title into something much bigger than it is: the rather wistful, moving film *Brief Encounter* becomes 'Really Long Encounter'; *Great Expectations*, by Charles Dickens, becomes 'Huge Expectations'. For #DogTitles, Emily Brontë's rather sombre classic *Wuthering Heights* becomes 'Wuthering Bites', Tolstoy's Russian epic *War and Peace* is 'War and Fleas', Virginia Woolf's

Hesitation

This game has many names – you might have heard a version of it on on a BBC Radio 4 called *Just a Minute*.

Everyone takes a few slips of paper and writes down some topics like 'The Weather', 'Flowers' or 'My Favourite Book'. Include some strange ones – 'Glue', 'Haircuts', 'Uncles', 'Fridges'. Then stick all the topics in a hat, give them a good mix-up.

Now take it in turns to pull out a topic and try to talk about it for one minute. It's harder than it sounds! It means speaking continuously, without repetition, deviation (going off-topic) or hesitation. Other players can accuse the speaker of doing one of the above by interrupting and – if the chairperson agrees – the person challenging takes over.

The winner is whoever is still speaking at the end of the time limit.

MARSUPIALS	CLEANING PRODUCTS
	GETTING STUCK IN A LIFT
	DISNEY MOVIES
THE NORTH POLE	
	MYTHICAL BEASTS

literary masterpiece *A Room with a View* becomes 'A Room with a Poo', Philip Pullman's *His Dark Materials* becomes 'His Bark Materials'. You get the idea? It is joyfully irreverent and playful and creative. And you can run with this almost endlessly – if you run out of book titles (unlikely), there are songs, films, plays and TV programmes. Why not try #FitnessTitles (think Bruce Willis's 'Diet Hard'), How about #illnesstitles ? 'One Flu Over the Cuckoo's Nest', #FoodTitles 'Omelette Prince of Denmark'? Or

#RuinAGoodTitleWithOneLetter? 'Breakfast at Toffany's'? 'Wind in the Pillows'? And then work on some other #Titles!

In the Hot Seat

We've talked about using existing materials as a jumping-off point for ad-libbing in the forms of the writing on the wall, signs, titles. We can also use long-form existing works for some more in-depth ad-libbing on a slightly more serious level. There comes a moment in the plot line of a story when the character expresses a feeling, about the situation or about themselves. The first well-developed example of this is Shakespeare's soliloquies. We reach a point in a play where the character is given the stage, to tell us what she or he is thinking: 'To be or not to be ...', 'Is this a dagger I see before me ...' and all that. Let's look at how we can work with these moments in a creative way.

I recently told some children the story of Hansel and Gretel. Now remember, if you tell the story in its original form, it's a tough tale. It's about two parents who are so poor that they abandon their children in the forest. In fact, they do it twice. The children overhear their parents planning it, so when it comes to the trip where they're going to be abandoned, Hansel has a trick prepared: as they walk deep into the forest, he drops stones on the ground, so after they've been left, they can follow the stones all the way back home. The second time they're abandoned, Hansel drops a trail of bread. But this time the birds eat it and the children find themselves lost at night in the middle of the forest where they could be attacked by wolves or wander about without food for days. The children could die. It is both a dangerous situation and one of terrible emotions: their parents have abandoned them twice – and this time there is no way home. This moment of high emotion and tension is perfect for ad-libbing.

If working in a group, you can do this using the technique of 'freeze frame' and 'hot seating'. Invite your group to enact a scene from a story, set yourselves up as if you are caught by a camera as you enact that scene and at the trigger moment hold it as a freeze-frame. Then you can then go around, with each person in the scene staying in character and describing what's on their mind at that moment. What people come up with are in effect the same kinds of speeches as soliloquies. The more intensely you involve yourself with the story, the more you think through the freeze-frame, the easier it is to come up with a good hot-seat speech.

This is not just a group activity. You can experiment with versions of this on your own while writing, acting, directing or just pausing as you read a story or watch a film. You can freeze-frame the scene in your mind, pick the character you're interested in and 'hot-seat' them. If you care about the story enough to be doing this, you will come up with some surprising insights into what's going on in that scene, with that character and maybe in the play or film as a whole. Why not try it with your favourite book or film that you've read or watched a hundred times, and I can guarantee you will find something new even in a familiar old favourite.

Now let's flip that on its head and do it all the other way round. What if, rather than being in an interpretive position, you're in a creative position – perhaps you're in a play, or you're writing a story. You're thinking about a character, you're building up motivation. You're playing with ideas to do with why a character is acting in a certain way, or perhaps you're still working out where the plot is going to take them.

One way into this is to hot-seat it again, by doing an 'improv' with yourself or with the actors. This might be in order to create some words for a sketch or drama that you're putting on, or in order to find reasons for a character's actions, or their facial expressions, body shapes, tone of voice. As before, you can do this by voicing the character's thoughts at that moment. And you can assist this by doing a bit of 'archaeology' into your character to find out more of their back-story, the stuff that happened to them before the story began. Ask questions of your character: what are their parents like? Has anything shocking or tragic happened in their life? Do they have brothers and sisters? What are their dreams or aspirations?

If you're working in a group, it's important to explore the group dynamics of a scene through improv. At first, try enacting a scene where nothing out of the ordinary happens, simply playing out how the characters each behave in the group environment – make it somewhere familiar and mundane, perhaps a crowded shop or café. Do you look up and smile at people, or do you look inwards and not say sorry if you bump into others? Are you polite or are you grumpy and rude? Do you hold yourself confidently or try and fade into the background? This improv provides us with a 'baseline' of how our character might behave as part of everyday life.

Now we can mix things up a bit, throw in a dilemma, a crisis, a disruptive event: someone has a medical crisis, or there's a theft, or an act of violence. Or perhaps someone does something entirely unexpected – they lie down on the pavement and start doing swimming actions, or start hopping around like a kangaroo, or suddenly speaking another language. Or maybe we are in magical realism territory, and something extraordinary happens: a giant flying flower appears in the sky, or there's a mysterious rain of sardines.

Even if the eventual scene you will act out is defined by a script and a plot – for example, a scene at Hogwarts from a Harry Potter script – playing about with improv informs the quality and depth of the characters – how they look, how they speak, how they move – and will make the scripted scene much stronger when you come to enact it.

Mapping a Movie

Look on Googlemaps or on a real map and pick five street names. Turn them into a book or film title, then come up with a brief description of the story. I found: School Lane, Butler Close, Fosse Way, Fox Hollies and Soar Brook. My key words here are School, Butler, Fosse, Fox/Hollies and Soar/Brook.

- *Soaring Fox* – 'The terrifying tale of a giant fox that terrorised the London suburbs.'

- *The School for Butlers* – 'A hilarious romp when a group of ex-convicts retrain to become butlers for the super-rich.'

- *The Haunting of the Hollies* – 'A ghostly thriller based in a botanical garden in upstate New York.'

Have a go at mapping a movie

-

-

-

-

-

There are also opportunities to play around with an existing script – why not? I once worked with the late John Doona, author and drama teacher, on the opening scenes from Shakespeare's *The Tempest*. There are two central moments here: the shipwreck at night and the following morning finding yourself marooned on a desert island. Shakespeare has written words for these two scenes, but we don't have to be confined by them. We can pick out some of them and we can invent others; we can make up songs or chants to express what our characters are feeling and experiencing. We started with the scenes as they were written and then moved on to the improvisations.

We began by thinking and talking about what we would see, hear, smell, taste and touch during the storm and the shipwreck. We talked about what kind of person we were – sailor, aristocrat or servant? We talked about why we were on this boat, what we wanted from the journey before we set out and how this affected our attitude to the storm. Were we afraid or full of bravado? Did we seek help and comfort from others or offer it?

Then we shifted tone and we were on a beautiful beach on a warm sunny morning, but the crew were scattered, each of us alone and fearing the worst for our companions. How did we feel now? Fear that our loved ones had drowned? What about the crew members that we hated, feared or were rivals with? We fed in the idea that comes up later in the play that the isle is full of noises, a thousand 'twangling' instruments seem to be playing in the air. We decided we needed some music creating a background to the scene.

After an hour or so of this, we ended up with something that was and wasn't *The Tempest*. It was one particular group of people's exploration of the themes and images in the play, using our own emotions, voices and bodies to express it.

Through engaging in improv – individually in our heads or in a rehearsal with other people – we discover new depths to the character that we are exploring, hidden motivations that might influence how they respond to the current situation. By the time you've worked through the character's background, their current emotional landscape, how they react in different scenarios, you will be acting or writing with more depth, more subtlety, and it might even take the story in a whole new direction.

Flytes of Fantasy

In some cultures and subcultures there are long traditions of verbal insult, of outdoing each other with boasts, tall stories, lies, shaggy-dog stories and the like. This has a rich tradition in literature, going back to Old Norse myths and the culture of 'flyting'. The word 'flyting' comes from 'quarrel', but the old flytings were more than a mere squabble: they were a showcasing of linguistic and verbal skill and prowess.

The most famous Norse flyting was between Loki, the mischievous god always out to cause trouble, and the rest of the Norse gods. Loki enters the hall where the other gods are feasting and proceeds to wreak havoc by verbally sparring with each and every god, picking up their weaknesses and flaws and throwing them in their faces. While Loki's flyting is a rather nasty piece of work, designed to offend and hurt (and ends badly for Loki, when the other gods imprison him in a cave for eternity), more playful examples of these verbal games can be found throughout history and across the globe. Flytings were played below ground by miners, particularly in the north-east of England. Folklorists went to the Appalachian mountains in the US to collect insult dialogues, and in songs and the patter between them you might come across an exchange like the following:

'You're so mean, if you had a doughnut you'd keep the hole.'

'Well really? I'll tell you something about yourself. You're so mean, that you take back your sausage skins to the butchers to have them filled.'

'Uh-huh? You're so forgetful there was that time you put your cat to bed and put yourself outside.'

The key to this game is the formula word 'so'. Once you get into the rhythm of it, you attach the word 'so' to descriptions of people, places, things, weather: 'You're so [blank] that you ...' or 'The weather's so [blank] round here that ...' etc. You'll notice that in the exchange above, each person is feeding off the comment of their opponent in a kind of verbal tennis, acknowledging the opponent's gambit, then outdoing it with their own.

As well as trading insults, the more playful of these games trade boasts or tall stories. To go back to our Appalachian friends, the conversation might lead to an exchange of increasingly fantastical claims:

'I know a man who's so strong, he can knock you up in the air so high, that you'll starve on the way down.'

'Yeah, is that so? I know a man who can run so fast he meets himself coming back.'

'Oh yeah? I know a man who's so good at jumping that he can jump across a river and back without touching the other side.'

Flytings were the precursor to many modern forms – such as the rap battle, where two rappers spar to outdo each other with verbal dexterity, in speed, rhyme and content. We see flyting pop up in poetry, like the childhood classic 'My Dad's Bigger Than Your Dad'. (You could make up your own daft ones: 'My dad's boots are bigger than your dad's boots.' 'My dad's big boots are dirtier than your dad's big boots.' 'My dad's big, dirty boots are smellier than your dad's big, dirty, smelly boots ...') Or in more mainstream popular culture such as TV and radio shows like *In a League of Their Own*, *The Unbelievable Truth*, *8 Out of 10 Cats Does Countdown* and *Would I Lie to You?*, where contestants try to outdo each other with bigger and better insults (or apparent insults – they are mainly in jest) or lies that become increasingly ridiculous.

The ridiculous nature of the insult, lie or boast is crucial. The more ludicrous, the better. The trick is to conjure up a moment

Two Tellers

Get into pairs. You're going to invent a story as you're telling it – and act it out as you go along!

Start off with 'Once upon a time ...' and then take it in turns to say the next word. Be ready for the story to take you in any number of weird directions!

of fantasy that is beautifully impossible, so extravagantly insulting that it ceases to be offensive because it is no longer seen to be a 'truth'. In a way it's a kind of storytelling.

A Tale as Old as Time

Some people can just tell stories. They just have the knack. I've known people with no professional storytelling in their lives, no experience of writing, acting or singing, but who can, given the right situation, spin out stories, particularly around a group of 'stock characters'. When my two youngest children were young, their grandmother was their top bedtime treat because she would tell long tales about someone called Sammy Squirrel. The children much preferred these to anything I might concoct in my self-consciously professional way. I'd hear peals of laughter coming from the bedroom – much, much more than I ever got from my carefully sculpted gags. She focused in on things that the children had done that day, and she wove them into the adventures and problems of Sammy Squirrel up in his tree house. As far as I know, Sammy Squirrel could go anywhere and do anything, but was liable to get himself into scrapes. She also made a point of putting the children themselves into the stories. They met up with Sammy Squirrel and did things with him. It was a wonderful example of how the storyteller spins their tale out of the people and moment at hand, and was just magical.

But how do you do it? One way, as I've said, is to weave people from the audience into the adventures. Another is to make use of stock characters – like Sammy Squirrel. The more stories you tell about your stock characters, the more they will grow and develop. You don't even have to create your own stories from scratch; you can recycle stories that are already in your head, retelling them and replacing the characters with members of your audience or from your supply of stock characters. Why not use a tried and tested old story like Cinderella, Dick Whittington, Puss in Boots or Little Red Riding Hood and insert a character from another story? What happens if Father Christmas turns up for Cinderella, rather than her fairy godmother? Does Rudolph drive her to the ball in her pumpkin coach? You don't even have to use the whole story; you can lift specific moments or 'motifs' from them. That's to say, take the moment in Cinderella where the stepmother and the sisters force Cinderella to clean up after them. That's a great motif to recycle because it's got obvious injustice at the heart of it. And you can flip these moments on their head, take a sad moment and make it funny or vice versa, from the way you tell it.

You can take this one step further and take a much longer story that you know, like, let's say, a Shakespeare play, a musical, an opera, or a novel like *Lord of the Rings*. Now you retell it, with your own twist. A particularly rich seam are 'quest' stories like the *Odyssey*, where Odysseus and his crew are coming back from a war and get waylaid by a series of mishaps because of the silly mistakes he makes. Don't laugh, but I transposed that basic story to the French countryside (we were on holiday in France at the time), and it was a mix of animals and insects on a long journey to the beach so that they could get a boat

Emotional Transfers

In pairs: one person acts out an emotion – let's say, sadness – while the other acts out another emotion – such as anger.

Now transfer your emotions slowly from one to the other.

Sad person slowly becomes angry person while at the same time angry person becomes sad person.

You have thirty seconds in which to do it.

to the Île de Ré (which we had visited on that holiday). The Odysseus character was Gaston Le Dog and he bade farewell to his beloved Araigneé the Spider. He gathered around him a variety of helpers like Libellule the Dragonfly, but there were dangers from LouLou the Wolf and Ours the Bear. It was the time of year when the owls were very vocal, so there were important roles for Hibou (the tawny owl) and Chouette (the little owl), who make very distinctive noises (it's good to build in as many of the senses as possible). The local landscape was full of dangers: bogs, cliffs, falling trees. There were clouds of Moustiques (mosquitoes) and the dreaded Frelons (hornets). Given that it was the countryside, it was easy to weave in a sufficient amount of danger from cow-poo and bulls farting. Gaston Le Dog and his companions were always talking about getting to the beach before heading back home to Araignée. Then there was a surprising pay-off. When they got to the beach, Araignée was already there. She didn't feel like waiting for Gaston to come back; she wanted to go to the Île de Ré too.

I'm getting quite misty-eyed here thinking about that. It went on for several weeks and over several holidays, and that is the beauty of a quest narrative: it can be contracted and expanded to last as long as you wish – or until you run out of mishaps.

Another simple tool to help with this kind of improvised storytelling, and you can make it a party game too, is the 'three-thing' trick. My daughter was particularly fond of this one. Here, one person comes up with three things that the other person has to weave into a story. Then the person tries to tell the story and they must, must use the things in creative and surprising ways. They can't just appear in a list. Then you swap over. The person thinking up the three objects should try to make them the least likely to appear together in a story as possible: a unicorn, a spaceship and a loaf of bread. Or a bottle of fizzy water, an octopus and Henry VIII. Again, I can feel myself getting quite sentimental remembering this, seeing the young woman my daughter is now as a quirky four-year-old thinking up crazy things for me to tell stories about.

Luckily for me, this is part of my professional life. I have been doing one-man poetry and story stand-up comedy shows for children and families for over forty years. I use poems and stories that are favourites and regulars, but I am always weaving in recent events, observations or memories that I've just dug up. With each telling, these grow and develop. Just like my dad adding embellishments to give shape, tension and comedy to his family stories, I do something similar. That's how my 'Chocolate Cake' poem took shape. I started off thinking of how my brother and I used to 'raid the larder' – that is, go to the cupboard and nick food. In real life my mother was very indulgent and took the attitude that if we were hungry we should eat, but that doesn't make for drama. I needed a bit of 'jeopardy', so I started to tell how Mum would get really angry. Then I thought of a bit more jeopardy – getting up in the middle of the night. But then, getting up to eat any old food is not very clear. Much better is to have something amazing and delicious: like chocolate cake. But not any old chocolate cake: special Mum chocolate cake. Now I could express that in words, but I had seen the wonderful Italian actor, playwright and raconteur Dario Fo doing an act of a poor peasant cooking a fly and pretending that it was a huge, scrumptious meal full

Crazy Spelling Test

Before you start, each player prepares by brainstorming a selection of crazy words.

Take it in turns to be the caller or the speller.

The caller calls out a word they've invented: 'Schnorple'.

The speller tries to spell it:

"S-C-H-N-O-R-P-L-E"

Then the speller comes up with a meaning:

Schnorple: to slurp soup with your face directly in the bowl.

The caller then acts this out.

There are no wrong answers. Whoever gets the most laughs wins.

HOST YOUR OWN FLYTING

It might be best to play it safe, and trade boasts rather than insults. Take it in turns with a partner to come up with bigger and better boasts – about how fast you can run, how high you can jump, how long your tongue is or clever your hair is (Einstein – now there's a man with clever hair). It can be anything – but the more ridiculous the better! And remember that formula, try and start with something like 'Yeah, well *my* ...' and then build on the other person's boast.

of glorious gloating sounds, and I thought I would lift some of that. Bit by bit, each time I performed the story I added in these different elements until I arrived at a shape. But even now I add bits. I've started adding a bit more jeopardy when I'm eating the cake, and I imagine that my parents are coming downstairs ...

More recently, I developed what would become the poem 'I was born in the Stone Age'.

Children often ask me how old I am
They look at me and say, 'You're SO OLD.
I mean YOU'RE REALLY OLD.
REALLY REALLY OLD.'
and I have to explain to them that

I was born in the Stone Age.
In the Stone Age
all we had was stones, rocks, pebbles
Grit, gravel ...
At home we didn't have chairs.
We sat on a rock.
'Mum it's really uncomfortable!
My bum hurts.'
'Shush!' she'd say, 'it's not the Chair Age yet.'

and so I go on ...

This began when I heard myself describing the two men who brought in our first TV set in 1956. Before that, we had no TV. Can you imagine? Then I start to exaggerate, the TV set becomes as big as a wardrobe (no flat-screens back then), but the screen is no bigger than a sandwich. And it's not colour TV, it's not even black-and-white. It's grey and grey ... When children heard this, they always asked me when I was born. I used to be direct and honest. I know my 'honest' voice, so I 'borrow' it in order to tell the most outrageous lies. Now, whenever a child asks me how old I am, I say, 'I was born in the Stone Age. I'm three thousand and [here I add my real age] years old.' And then I go off on an improvised thing about how everything we had in the Stone Age was made of rock. We ate rocks for tea. We didn't have a TV, we just watched a rock. And then we went to bed – which was also a rock. At school the teacher would say, 'Take out your rock', and we had to write on it with a little rock, called a 'stone' ... And so on and so on.

In this way a poem grew from live ad libs. I tell the children it's like when you watch someone making candyfloss. You see the stick gathering up more and more fluffy stuff. That's how I make up these improvised poems and stories.

Lend Me Your Ears

The very art of storytelling has its origins in improvisation and ad-libbing. Storytelling pre-dates the written word, and is hundreds of years older than the printing press. Incredibly, wonderfully, the oldest stories, like the *Odyssey*, *Beowulf* and the Icelandic sagas, were made up, remembered and adapted orally by bards who carried great treasure troves of stories

#Titles

Pick a theme, here are some suggestions:

#DogTitles

#CatTitles

#LittleTitles

Now adapt film, song, play, book or TV show titles to suit the new theme. So, for #DogTitles, you could have *The Hound of Music*, or for #CatTitles *The Great Catsby* or *Richard the Purred*. For #LittleTitles you could have *The Small Lebowski* or *Stuart Little-r...* Get others to join in online and use a hashtag to follow the responses.

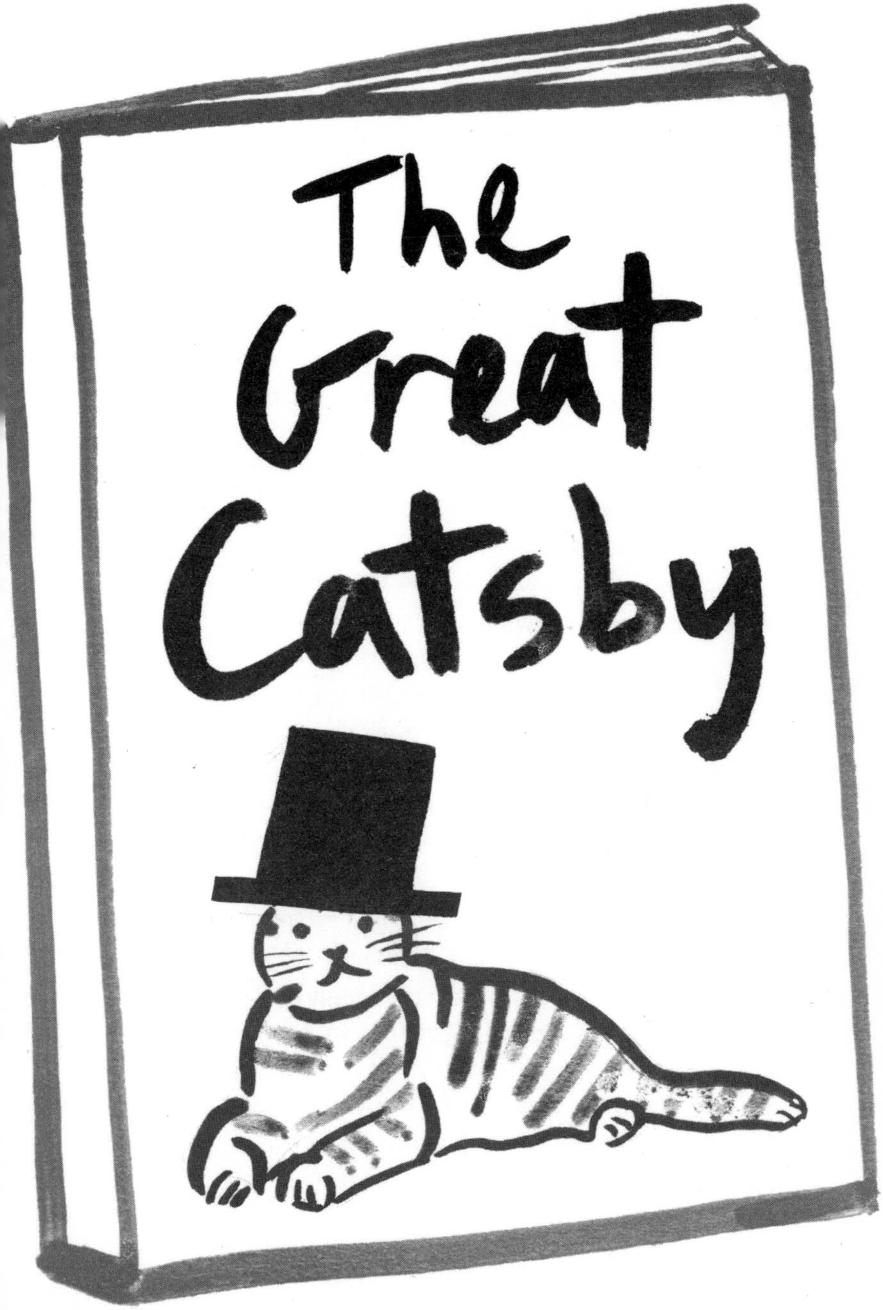
The Great Catsby

in their heads. By doing some very clever statistical analysis, scholars have shown that great swathes of the stories that have come down to us are based on what they call 'oral formulae'. The formulae are short chunks of just two or three words, a phrase that the bard can drop into a line, which then links to another formula to tell the next part; in this way the stock phrases form the unchanging skeleton of a story. The bard doesn't have to 'compose' in the way that most writers write novels, where they are often trying to come up with original and individual ways of expressing things. For the bards it was quite the opposite: their descriptions, similes, metaphors and many other elements of the story are orally remembered clichés that they have stashed in their memory like a treasure trove waiting to be opened up and poured out one after the other. On reading such epics nowadays, it seems incredible and improbable that people could remember so much.

The bards were then free to ad-lib around the formulaic skeleton of the story. It was not a totally free-form storytelling, but, as we've explored in this chapter, ad-libbing is often in fact working with a tool kit of pre-existing material, and many modern storytellers and rappers do something very similar. They hold in their head the outlines of hundreds of stories or rhymes. And if you dig down another level, within these outlines are hundreds, if not thousands, of phrases, which express images, actions, feelings, thoughts. These can be called up when the progress of the story, or rap, naturally stimulates them. And every time this great pool of language is being used, new ideas, phrases or images will pop up and be tried out. If they work, if the audience likes it, they may well get put into the pool for use again. And it's not just the storyteller who can do this; someone listening in the audience might think, 'I could reuse that, I could use that for my story or rap or poem about the time we were caught in a blizzard ...'. That's how oral story, song and poetry develop. And it all goes back to the *Odyssey* and before.

Taking Stock

As I've mentioned, I once saw a performance by Dario Fo. One particular section worked with commedia dell'arte, a form of improvised Italian comedy dating back to the sixteenth century, which works from 'stock characters': most famously, the greedy old man Pantalone and the harlequin Arlechino. Commedia dell'arte was immensely popular, and when the sixteenth-century audiences went to see the plays they would already know a lot about the characters; sometimes they would know the plot line, but sometimes it would be a new one. They knew that at various points there would be verbal or physical lazzi, quick-fire, repetitive sequences that would dazzle the audience. Some of the words would be familiar, but others would be new and surprising. And some of the dialogue would clearly be ad-libbed because it was a response to something shouted out from the audience – the art of heckling is just as old as the ancient art of theatre!

These plays were built up through improvisations. They would start from basic plot lines and situations, and dialogue would be inserted according to what was appropriate for the

Thinking on your Feet

Blindfold yourself and make a scribble on a blank page.
Remove the blindfold: you have five minutes to turn your
initial mark into a drawing of something recognisable – such
as a face or a machine or an animal. Try and make it as
imaginative as possible!

Animal Fair

What do you think my dangaroo looks like? Can you turn other words into animals? Here are a few words to get you started on a mythical menagerie:

- Hippocampus (actually, it's part of your brain to do with memory!)
- Paradox
- Humbug
- Gazillion
- Interlope

Can you describe them, draw them? Where do they live? What food do they eat?

stock character in each situation – sometimes this would be rehearsed, sometimes improvised. The stock characters provided the solid basis for this: the mean old man would be mean, the sad clown would be sad, the vulgar clown would be vulgar, the two clowns would be in love with the girl, the doctor would be full of scholarly nonsense knowledge and the captain would seem to be brave but in reality wasn't, and so on. The troupes would tour, do shows at fairs and festivals, updating their plays with topical and regional references, weaving in music and dance, outdoing each other's verbal and physical lazzi. We see traces of this in modern panto, with the stock figures of the pantomime dame, the sad and vulgar clown figures, in the lazzi in the laundry room with Wishee-Washee or Widow Twankey. Good panto actors will work in good ad libs from rehearsals, or even from performances as the show runs.

You can see traces of commedia in Shakespeare's use of stock characters. The Captain figure from commedia appears as Pistol in *Henry IV Part II*. Perhaps there are traces of the Doctor figure in Polonius in *Hamlet*. Meanwhile, we might say that the bawdy Nurse in *Romeo and Juliet* is a perfect match for her commedia counterpart, Colombina. In *Twelfth Night*, Feste is a classic example of the sad clown figure who we usually call in Britain by the French name Pierrot. And there is plenty of reason to think that Shakespeare left some of the fool scenes unwritten, so that a professional clown like Robert Armin could ad-lib or use their old ad libs in those scenes.

This little run-down reminds us that Shakespeare was a great recycler of dramatic treasures that were at hand. He wove together traditions from Ancient Rome and Greece, contemporary Italy, old historical chronicles, the Bible, pagan myths, legends and beliefs and much more. In a way, he (and his team of players) were great improvisers, grabbing whatever tools were available and knocking them together.

Finally, a quick word on the latest form of ad-libbing: freestyling. I've seen everyone from teenagers, professional rappers, DJs and even the boxer Anthony Joshua trying this. What you do is have a rap rhythm in your head – maybe it's a four-beat line – with little off-beats in between. You start up saying something about what you're doing, where you've been, why or how you're having a great time, and all the time, in the back of your mind, you're thinking of the things around you that rhyme or nearly rhyme. Anthony Joshua was thinking of his training, so he was finding rhymes in 'steps' , 'reps', 'flex'.

Can you think how that might go?

This is not his version, I'm just remembering the rhymes: something like this:

> All of the time I'm doing my reps
> Eating up the road, doing my steps
> Getting in the gym, see the muscle flex
> Building up the quads, building up me pecs ...

The key to this way of ad-libbing is preparing by having a stock of rhymes in your head, and while you're actually doing the rap, you have to think ahead. The best way to start is to be not too ambitious. Just think of one couplet and a chorus

Stealing Stories

The simplest and easiest way to make up a story is to steal one and change things to make it your own.

You could change:

- the time frame – set the story in a different era;

- the location – set the story somewhere else;

- the characters – men become women, people become animals or a mixture of the two;

- or you could add a subplot.

Tell your story, and see if anyone can guess what the original was.

that you can keep coming back to. If the rap is about you, you can do something like:

> I know who I am, I know that I'm me;
> You know what you get, it's what you see.

That's the bit you can repeat. Around that, you can put 'couplets' – two lines that rhyme – about what kind of person you are.

And that's the end of my very short freestyle lesson, from – you might think – the most unlikely, inappropriate person to be giving the lesson – a middle-aged white guy, born in the Stone Age! But doesn't that tell you something? The great thing about play is that it overcomes age, class and race – if you want. And we can all learn from each other. Can't we?

The End

What have we learned? What have we got in the tool kit?

Ad-libbing doesn't necessarily mean inventing things from scratch. You can work with what is a kind of mind library, a pool of stock words, phrases, characters, rhymes.

You can shuffle and juggle with these. You can turn them round to see what happens.

You can surprise yourself.

You can take scenes from real life and inject fibs, exaggerations, jeopardy into them to make them grab audiences or make yourself laugh.

If you look around you, the world is full of stuff to go in your tool kit: signs, jokes you overhear on buses, snatches of what people say on TV, styles of talking – anything.

Often the things that catch the eye or ear are surprising juxtapositions – the strange with the familiar.

People love to hear the familiar made unfamiliar. People love to hear about the unfamiliar that you bring to them – just like my dad did with the journey over the moors.

Reflect on what you say. How did that work? Why didn't that one work so well?

Is that a tool kit?

What do you think?

What else do you think it needs?

Make a Book!

Take your storytelling to the next level and make a book.

The simplest way is to take a sheet of A4, fold it once, fold it again and then slit open the folded tops of the 'pages' – you'll have eight pages (sides) to play with. You could be conventional and use the front and back as the 'covers'. You could use inside the front and back for some kind of design. You could put a title page on side 3 and then write on, draw on, stick photos (and cut-outs) on and design all the other sides.

You could invent a new kind of book, starting in the middle and working outwards.

Or make concertina books. Take an A4 sheet, and cut it down the vertical middle. Fold the two strips into a concertina and stick them together. Now you can write, draw, paint on or stick photos and cut-outs on these surfaces. Concertina books are also good for cutting through the pages to create 'windows' so you can see through the next page.

What kind of book will you write?

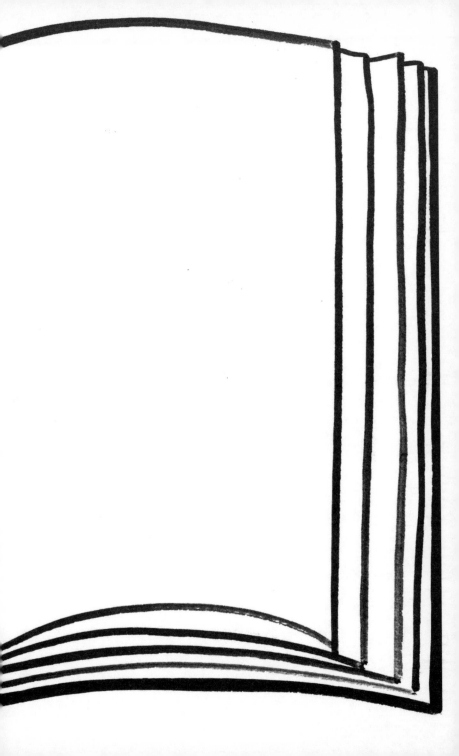

To Infinity and Beyond...

When I was a boy, we lived in a flat over a shop. Out the back was a yard, about 3 by 3 metres square, and along one side was a coal bunker. It was about 2 metres long and a metre and a half high, with two hatches in its roof and a little doorway at the front. The men from the coal lorries tipped the coal through the hatches, and we shovelled coal out for our fires through the little door in the front.

When the bunker was nearly empty, my brother and I often climbed in and acted out stories from the war, imagining that it was an air-raid shelter, a tank, a Spitfire or a submarine. When you were inside, you could open a hatch and poke your head out, as if you were in a cockpit or a tank turret, or coming up after a night in the shelter after a bombing raid. Bombing raids had happened up until just two years before I was born. All the adults I knew had lived through that time.

Once I came home early from school, climbed into the bunker by myself and headed off into outer space. I should say here that this was several years before the first manned space flight and the moon landing. I took off in my spaceship and a short while later climbed into the control tower by pushing open the hatch. I started to deliver orders, describing what I could see floating through space, sending back messages to base on earth. There were some quite severe problems to face – wandering meteorites, a failed engine, oxygen contamination – but I pressed on. I think I had been going with this running commentary for at least ten minutes when I scanned the star-strewn horizon, only to find that my father was standing by the back fence watching me. He had been listening in to my dramatised monologue for quite a while. I stopped. He said how much he had enjoyed it, treating it as though it had been some kind of comedy routine. I can remember being a bit embarrassed about it, as though I had done something naive or childish.

But what was I doing?

The name we give this is 'role-play' or 'dramatic play', and it is fairly common among young children but tends to fade away as children get older. Not all children do it, and it is variously encouraged or discouraged depending on who is looking after the children. No one ever discouraged it in our house – quite the opposite: my parents were very keen on theatre, produced plays at the schools they taught at and they each told stories about their lives in ways that dramatised what had happened, filling them with dialogue and actions. My brother often had the job of looking after me, filling the gap between the end of school and my parents coming home from work. These hours were filled with games, chat, stories and jokes, and as my brother was a great mimic of authority figures, he could act being his teachers, our parents or just random people we had met. We could slip very easily from him entertaining me by mimicking real life into a fantasy world of dramatic play or 'make-believe' – often involving the coal bunker.

Why do children play these games? Why was I in the bunker going to space?

Professionals who comment on childhood and play place different emphases on its various aspects, but for some the most important aspect of dramatic play is that it is a symbolic medium. What I mean by this is that the play represents things. The whole thing depends on pretending. Part of the essence of being human is that we learn (or we are taught) how to symbolise what's around us. In dramatic play, a child does this through making an object standing in for something otherwise unattainable: it might be something based on a child's experience of the real world – a box forming a pretend shop, a tunnel for toy cars made out of loo-roll insides – or it might be more fantastical, like a coal bunker standing in for a space rocket. This ability to project an idea onto a physical object teaches a child something valuable; as we grow up, we increasingly have to rely on symbol systems to understand and navigate the world around us. Language is perhaps the most important of our symbol systems. When we say 'sky', the word itself is not the sky – it 'represents' it, so that we are able to talk about the sky abstractly. In this chapter we are going to explore the different things, emotional, physical and fantastical, that are symbolised and represented in dramatic play.

Emotional Charades

Give classic Charades a twist and, instead of using books or films, try acting out emotions for your audience, without using any words.

You can try this with abstract words too.

Or colours? How are you going to act out 'red'?

Remember, the audience have to do as much work here as the actor – half the game is in the guessing!

'Tis But a Dream

As children, our ability for make-believe is truly astonishing. Our young brains have a higher degree of plasticity, and neural connections are still forming, making us highly creative and adaptable – or at least, that's the scientific explanation I've been given. But what is astonishing is just the sheer amount of imagination we have, and it enables our young selves to see possibilities everywhere. Dramatic play is often a child's first foray into exploring that creativity and pushing the boundaries. As yet, they don't have much experience of how the world works 'in real life', so why can't that big dog be a woolly mammoth? Why can't the sheet over the table create a cave of wonders? Why can't the tall grass be an enchanted forest? With some imagination – this is all possible!

Make-believe is an opportunity for all of us to expand our horizons and operate outside the limits of normal life. In make-believe we can go anywhere! See anything! Be anyone! If you can be anything, where would you go? Who would you like to be? Perhaps you'd like to see the horsehead nebula, 1,500 light years from earth, or be the Pharaoh Tutankhamun, or be able to fly or breathe under water ... For me, it was taking a rocket into outer space. If I hadn't noticed my dad watching, who knows what mysterious planets I might have gone on to discover, what strange extraterrestrial beings I might have met? Or my favourite dream thing – giant asteroids that held inside them mysterious civilisations.

While flights of fancy like this might seem beyond us as adults, something we dismiss as 'childish', there are ways that we still indulge in a little make-believe – such as the joy of a good daydream! Do you ever allow your mind to wander off? Perhaps it starts with your current scenario – sitting in your office, walking through the park or cooking – and spins off from there, or perhaps it's altogether more fantastical. Daydreaming like this, allowing your brain a little make-believe, is not only very enjoyable but may have real benefits: the complex problem-solving areas of the brain are active when we daydream, suggesting it could be helping us to creatively think our way through a current problem or situation; daydreams can help with consolidating something we've learned that day, working it into invented scenarios; and daydreaming may improve our working memory. So go ahead, have yourself a little daydream and don't hold back – take a trip to the moon, or the future colony on Mars, or the bottom of the sea. We'll see you when you get back.

(When children ask me for my main tip for writing poetry, I always says, 'daydream'.)

All Work and No Play...

As adults, our daydreams and make-believe may be more likely to centre on real-world situations. Interestingly, children are also very likely to engage in dramatic play that explores the 'real world' around them, although it is often a world as alien to them as the surface of the moon or the bottom of the sea – the world of grown-ups. What do they do all day? What happens at the mysterious 'office'? What is happening when you hear the chink of glasses downstairs, or the mutter of conversation, after 'lights out'? What is the purpose of a 'tie'?

Kids often re-enact dramatic situations based on their real life – tea-time, going to the doctors, going to play group or school, going on holiday – or on snippets of what they've seen of the grown-up world – going to work, going on a journey, running a shop. I know of one little girl who announced to her parents that she was off to the kitchen 'to burn the food', which says it all really! Children are such keen observers and constantly trying out what they've noticed about the adult world.

As well as the day-to-day grown-up world, dramatic play gives children the opportunity to explore the tide of current events which filter down to them but often remain puzzling and a little scary. When I took my coal-bunker rocket off to space it was the 1950s, and 'big' technology was the story of the moment. But we were being fed two opposing narratives about it. On the one hand, it was presented to us as very buzzy and exciting: a new frontier. On the other hand, there was an uneasy sense that this was World War Three – this time with spaceships. In fact, media analysts have a lot of fun interpreting the space literature and films of the 1950s in terms of lived-out fantasies of both the Second World War and the Cold War, which we were then going through.

In the 1940s and '50s the Second World War, which our parents had just been through, was presented to us British children as a tale of British pluck, against all the odds, defeating a ruthless, technologically superior foe – the version that we received was in many ways narrativised and turned into a story not unlike the make-believe dramas that we played out as kids! The Cold War we were going through right at that moment was presented to us as a conflict in which we were faced with a foe who made life hell for its citizens and who wanted to impose this terrible way of life on us and our rather lovely existence. Space was an arena in which this drama was played out in comics, radio and TV programmes and films. There was also an element of the old imperial mindset at work – underneath all this was the narrative of the British Empire (when 'we' were great) and how space would offer us a new frontier in which 'we' would revive our greatness, defeating hostile natives ('aliens') and colonising newly discovered planets. The means by which all this took place was the hugely powerful 'big' technology of rockets and spaceships, some of which had originated in the Second World War and was still being developed. You can see how the lines between fact and fiction could become blurred for children, as the narratives we heard about the 'real' world became confused with the narratives of film, TV and comic strips.

Much of this was a cause of anxiety among children, and yet there were hardly any spaces in which we could voice it. In school, every British invention or technological breakthrough was welcomed and celebrated. We sensed that it proved we were up with the Americans and Russians. As I poked my head out of the hatch and headed off beyond Mars, I think I was both part of this triumphalist narrative but also expressing my anxiety about it. I could express my desire to be bigger, better, stronger, more like the astronauts that were the heroes of the

After the 'Happily Ever After'

This is the Sequel and Prequel game.

Pick a fairy tale and imagine what happens *after* the end of the story.

What's going on three years after Cinderella married Prince Charming?

What did Goldilocks say to her mum when she got home?

If you know your Shakespeare: what do Ariel and Caliban do on the island now that Prospero and the rest have gone?

You can also turn this on its head and play 'backstories' – I often find the villains are the best characters for this. What made Snow White's stepmother so wicked – what happened in her life?

Gather a group of friends and cast them in your prequel–sequel stories.

current narrative, while at the same time using the 'play' to manage my fears. I was playing with ideas and questions that I didn't feel were being answered in the narrative provided: what was 'out there'? What was it all for? Where would it lead? Were there creatures out there who were trying to eliminate us, just as the Nazis had tried and the Russians were apparently trying to do now? Did 'we' have enough resources to keep us safe? Through dramatic play I could act out the different scenarios to answer these questions and perhaps lessen my anxieties about the real world.

It's worth considering what today's children are worrying about – or worrying through – in their play. They hear snippets of news about momentous issues such as environmental degradation and refugee crises. In some cases, they are more concerned than we realise. Research shows that children are more aware of climate change, for example, than their parents and teachers. We might just see that pop up in their play, as well as more immediate concerns about school and family. Children's mental health charity Place2Be has found that 56 per cent of children say they worry 'all the time', but that play is a powerful way to understand and access that anxiety.

Playing like this is a form of emotional education. Children put their anxieties, fears, desires, hopes onto the characters they play, onto the toys they animate or onto the counterparts they try to direct. Previously internalised feelings are taken out of this closet and into the open air, where they are 'tried out' in full daylight – but under the guise of make-believe.

The psychoanalyst Melanie Klein, a contemporary of Sigmund Freud, thought that this childhood act of playing out internalised anxieties had a powerful therapeutic role. Her area of expertise was trauma in children and trying to help children and families who experienced it. Traditionally, the method of psychoanalysis was 'the couch': sessions in which the 'analysand' (the client) lay on a couch and talked about whatever they wanted to talk about. The theory was (and still is) that at some point the person would find their way to moments of crisis in their lives that would 'explain' why they were experiencing the difficulty or problem they were going through. While this might (or might not) work for adults, it's not convenient, ethical or practical to do something similar with children – a different form of expression needed to be found. Melanie Klein devised games to play with children that she claimed could reveal the fundamental basis for the crisis that the child was experiencing. While a child might not be able to express their distress directly, either out of fear or simply because they do not have the words for what they have experienced, what Klein found was that if she put dolls, toys, toy animals and Plasticine in front of a child showing signs of trauma and asked the child to tell a story using the dolls and the other materials, the child would often 'play out' moments that typified the crisis or represented it.

Margaret Lowenfeld was another pioneer of what we now call 'play therapy'. The idea has become so commonplace that it's hard to imagine what a stir she and other trailblazers, such as Klein, caused when they put forward their theories about the therapeutic significance of play. Lowenfeld developed a specific tool called 'sandplay', which is exactly what it says on the tin, and is also known, more wonderfully, as World Technique. Using trays of wet and dry sand, plus lots of small toys and figures, children create their own worlds. The child is in control of their own world, their own story, with a therapist looking on and observing as a companion, rather than a guide. Lowenfeld believed that play was how children communicate, that it is their own non-verbal language. The child can decide which toy, figure, symbol or feeling comes to the fore and when.

A Walk on the Wild Side

Let's talk about monsters.

Melanie Klein was interested in the figurative 'monsters' that children might be struggling with, and which could be given form and expression through dramatic play. Monsters, both scary and friendly, feature in a lot of dramatic play, and we catch glimpses of this in stories for children too. In *Where the Wild Things Are*, by Maurice Sendak, the little boy Max dresses up in a wolf suit, becoming the monster himself, and says to his mother 'I'll eat you up!' – a classic line of aggression that children might express. As a result, Max is sent to his room without anything to eat. But from his bedroom he 'sails away' to the land of the Wild Things, big, ugly monsters who say that they want to eat Max – now the roles and reversed and Max discovers what it would feel like to be on the receiving end of the very same aggression that he expressed towards his mother.

This is an example of how dramatic play can help a child learn empathy, putting themselves in the position of someone else and viewing their own behaviour from a distance, assessing and experiencing how the other person might feel about their actions. It's also a story about overcoming monsters – the hungry beasts that start out so scary end up crowning Max as King of the Wild Things, and, fortunately for Max, at the end of the book he makes it home safely to his bedroom, where a hot supper appears – so no one has to be 'eaten up' after all!

A similar theme emerges in *Not Now, Bernard*, by David McKee. Bernard is a small boy who keeps warning his parents that there is a monster in the garden and it's going to eat him up. No matter how many times he says this, neither of his parents takes any notice. Sure enough, Bernard goes into the garden and the monster eats him up. The monster comes into the house and tries to attract the attention of the parents but they ignore him too. Who is this monster, and what does he represent? There are many possibilities: perhaps the monster is what a child might wish to be if a parent or parents go on and on and on ignoring them – the monster is more powerful than the child but also more powerful, ultimately, than the parents, and is able to show a level of aggression (eating everyone up!) that children are taught is not allowed. The child might wish aggressively that they could eat their parents up, both to eliminate them and to have them, in just the same way as we might say is going on with Max in *Where the Wild Things*

Would You Rather

This is a classic game that seems to become more popular with people as they get older. The key is to go as ludicrous as possible – and make sure there are some truly tough decisions in there!

Would you rather ...

- only be able to talk in rhyme or never, ever stop talking?

- have no teeth or only ever have liver-flavoured toothpaste?

- have a frog for a hand or always have a fly on the end of your nose?

- have one eye that always saw an hour into the future or a nose that smelled an hour into the past?

- have Charles Dickens as a pet or have Shakespeare talking all the time in your hearing aid?

Hint: You can play this so that one person does the first half of the question and someone else does the second.

Are. Not Now, Bernard is a make-believe expression of a child saying, 'Even if I was a monster you would ignore me, but then ... haha ... if I was a monster I could punish you for that, because I could eat you up, and then you would be sorry that you ignored me.'

In *The Gruffalo*, Julia Donaldson gives us a tiny mouse who fends off all the predators in the 'deep, dark wood', including the eponymous monster, with his wit and quick thinking. In fact, the mouse is ad-libbing and exaggerating like mad, using a lot of the tool kit we explored in Chapter 3! He seems to dream the Gruffalo into being in all his knobbly-kneed, warty glory, a power we often hope (or fear) we might have as children. (Who didn't spend hours staring furiously at an inert glass of water after reading *Matilda* for the first time?) Even the Gruffalo ends up terrified of the mouse, who has become 'the scariest creature in the wood', and in the topsy-turvy world of the story children see how they too might be powerful or have influence, all the while enjoying Donaldson's delightfully grisly imagery – 'roasted fox' and 'owl ice cream' – and thrilling subversion.

The Shrinking of Treehorn, by Florence Parry Heide, explores similar territory, with a child who is slowly shrinking while the parents ignore what is happening. The symbolic role-play here is that being ignored makes us feel diminished, and here the ignoring is represented by physical shrinking. Through Treehorn's shrinking the parents are being 'punished', as their child is being eliminated by their indifference. Unlike Bernard (who is ultimately eaten by his parents' indifference), Treehorn returns to 'normal' size and the book has a happy ending. In that sense the book seems to play out more a kind of warning rather than a metaphorical punishment. Alternatively, the book holds within it the possibility for a child who would like to shrink, who would like to be less visible. We can, of course, hold both ideas in our head at the same time: to resent being ignored and to want to be ignored! Again the book is a kind of role-play – and acts out exactly the fears about elimination and rejection that Melanie Klein was encouraging children to express through dramatic play as a form of therapy. Reading is in itself a form of role-play, where a child – or adult! – can play at being all kinds of different characters and versions of themselves and see how it makes them feel.

Stories like the three explored above are said to 'contain' the child. That's to say, a child may have feelings that are uncomfortable, contradictory, overwhelming or that the child is obsessed by. They may give voice to antagonisms and aggressions that the child can't control. One argument claims that a story (or role-play) engages a child by putting the child metaphorically 'inside' the situations and characters of the story. The story or role-play becomes a safe place in which feelings can be 'outed'. The role-play or story is not real, the character who is taking part, speaking, making decisions and acting on those decisions is not the 'real you' but can give voice or action to feelings you might be experiencing. Your feelings about whether these are right or wrong things to be doing or thinking, your hopes and fears about what it is the characters are doing and saying, are then 'contained' by the play or story, and so can be explored safely and without real-world consequences.

We might say tentatively that role-play and stories offer blueprints for possible ways of doing, thinking and speaking – and for ways of feeling. Within the role-play's new world you might allow yourself to feel angry and fierce or alternatively, gentle, vulnerable and soft, or indeed any other feeling that is taboo or impossible in your real life. This opportunity isn't just the preserve of childhood. In 2018 prisoners from HMP Spring Hill starred in a drama about the housing crisis and its very personal consequences, called *Broken Dreams: When Life Gives You a Fish*, at the Royal Court Theatre in London. They worked with the Kestrel Theatre Company, and its artistic director, Arabella Warner, has written passionately about how drama allowed the men to laugh, play, lose their inhibitions and shed 'the debilitating carapace of playing the hard man'. This work of art also challenges the audience and onlookers' perception of prisoners and who they might be or become.

Equally, this means that the role-play or stories don't have to be 'realistic' with characters from the 'real' world, such as teachers or parents (or colleagues or friends); they can be fantasies of any kind, with giants, or fairies or goddesses – so long as there is room for us to wonder about right and wrong, fair or unfair, safe or unsafe, sensible or not sensible and so on.

The Spectator

Dramatic play is often our first foray into the world of empathy and putting ourselves in another's position. We all have to learn, at some stage, that other people feel, think and emote just as we do – albeit in their own unique way – and this is a huge leap. Experts suggest that children don't usually develop the ability to empathise until they are about five years old. In dramatic play the child is both doing the action and being the audience, it enables a child to spectate itself – by 'becoming' a character they can direct and watch how that character responds and reacts to situations. This is also true when children spectate drama in stories, films, TV programmes, songs and the like. Part of the process is seeing that the kind of emotion expressed by a person in the drama might be similar to one in that child's own life. Importantly, spectating drama is not as passive as might at first appear – it is in fact another form of dramatic play. It's a complex web of responses in which we project our hopes and wishes onto the action and characters in the action. We make analogies between the things we know from our own lives and the things we see going on in the drama. These are what we might call 'acts of comparison', and as such they are the seeds we use to arrive at generalisations, categories and abstract thought.

I remember reading the Greek myth of Persephone and the Pomegranate Seeds to my daughter. When it comes to the moment when Persephone and her mother are separated, she called out, 'O I didn't want that to happen'. She brought her own experience of not liking separation from loved ones to bear on the action in the Greek myth. She had two examples now of that feeling of loss, grief and fear of separation: one from her own life and the one in the Greek myth. She could compare them. Later in the story we read that Persephone feels 'pity' for Pluto, the god of the underworld. My daughter asked,

THE MONSTER MASH

Draw a monster made out of things you're scared of –
perhaps it has the body of an Excel spreadsheet and
the legs of a spider, or the head of a dog and feet made
out of emails.

Be as abstract as you like. Then change the monster
into something you find funny. If it's got snakes for legs,
make it wear socks. (Did you know that snakes can't
move if they're wearing a sock?)

what is 'pity'? We talked about what it means to feel sorry for someone, just as you might feel sorry for your younger brother if he falls over. Here 'pity' is the abstract word, the category for a particular kind of emotion. There were two examples of pity for my daughter to consider here: the exchange of emotion between Persephone and Hades, and the other between my daughter and her younger brother. Making the analogy between the two was a first step towards understanding and handling an abstract. At some point further down the line she would be in a good position to consider 'pity' in contrast to, let's say, 'envy' or 'anger', or alongside what she experienced emotionally when she said, 'O I didn't want that to happen!' For her it was a very early experience of both empathy and abstraction. This way we build up understandings of the world and relationships beyond our own personal ones.

Dramatic play is part of the process by which we can do this, particularly in these situations in which we 'play out' relationships, spectating ourselves in the midst of action, moving around roles, altering outcomes, making comparisons. Let's say I think my mother is favouring my sister, then when I am role-playing at mums and dads (a common role-play among children), in my game I can take the role of my mother, my sister or me. I may pretend to be a mother who says to two dolls that I love this one more than that one. Or I might play the 'ideal' mother who treats both exactly the same, acting out a character that I believe to be much nicer than my real mother! Or I may play the child who I think is treated more favourably, and make her into an enemy, or perhaps just enjoy playing that role for a while. In this way, I inhabit each of the different roles and see the situation from different perspectives.

Each of these roles gives me the space and time to enable me to 'play out' what I think and feel in a symbolic way. If I role-play this game with others, I can similarly 'try out' being my mother, sister or myself up against someone else playing the counterparts. If you listen to children doing this, you will hear them asking each other for the chance to switch roles: 'Can I be the mummy now?' Or you'll hear the 'actors' telling each other how they want the other person to act: 'And then you start crying ...' 'And then I say, "If you don't do as I tell you, you're going to bed with nothing to eat."' And so on. In fact, this kind of provisional role-play can go on longer than a straight role-play. It's almost as if they never get to the action of the play because they are so immersed in the 'directing' of the action. You can see the pleasure children get from making these roles and actions so obviously changeable and playing with the idea of directing and influencing others. 'No you're not angry. You start laughing ...'

Play can lighten tense situations and lessen our fear, because we've practised or prepared already. I know of one boy adopted into a very loving family as a toddler. He had been through a lot in his young life, and was utterly terrified of Christmas: the noise, the brightness, the excess, the massive social expectations. So every year, from the very beginning of December, he and his family 'play Christmas'. They put on Christmas jumpers, play festive music and pull crackers. He can do what he likes: shout, cry, laugh like crazy – all within the game and with his parents close at hand. There are no negative consequences. It's just play: important, profound and transformative. By the big day itself, with all its potential stress, he's relaxed and ready to enjoy his role in the festivities.

Hypothetical

Challenge you friends with a what-if scenario they have to solve. Here are a few ideas to get you started:

- Travel round the world using as many modes of transport as possible, BUT you are starting out with zero money.

- You have been commissioned to write a musical about the life of a famous person such as Charles Darwin or Oprah Winfrey – you can use songs by any artists you like to illustrate this person's life. Take us through your script and playlist.

- You have been asked to cook a feast for Beyoncé's 100th birthday. You can only use ingredients or come up with dishes, foods and decorations that link to her songs. What are you going to make?

In his book, *Playful Parenting*, psychologist Lawrence Cohen talks about the way play, as well as building a child's emotional repertoire and resilience, has an important role in building connections between us, in cementing our attachments. He puts it like this:

> Play is children's main way of communicating. [...] To control every minute of their play is like controlling every word someone says. But to leave children all alone in their play is like spending the day with other adults and never talking to them.

You can nurture closeness by playing together, in other words. That's one element of trying on all those different hats in role-play: asking 'Who am I? Who am I when I'm with you? Who are we together?' Finding your identity as an individual and a member of a community.

If you're a natural history fan, you'll have noticed this kind of play everywhere in the animal world. When you've seen lion cubs together, you'll have noticed how they stalk, wrestle and pounce on one another. They are getting to know each other, which is essential to their later survival. The females work out and prefigure how they will hunt together as adults, and the males cement bonds that may be a matter of life or death against rivals in future.

Animals, like us, play to reconnect with each other when a connection has been severed or strained. While adult chimpanzees have a well-recognised set of reconciliatory behaviours, including cuddling and kissing, juveniles use their own language: they play. After a fight, one chimp will often approach another displaying a deliberate 'play face', tapping their knuckles on the floor, and a wild and exuberant time of rough and tumble inevitably follows. The troop need one another, and young chimps must find their place within it in order to survive. Furthermore, scientists like primatologist Frans de Waal are sure that many animals can empathise and respond to distress in others of their kind – empathy nurtured, no doubt, through play.

Walk a Mile in Another's Shoes

Returning to humankind, one key way for children to explore empathy through dramatic play is, as any teacher of very young children will tell us, to have a 'dressing-up box'. A set of hats, jackets, dresses, coats in a box will nearly always be enough to enable young children to get into a role. Each item of clothing can very quickly take on a transformative function. A hat or feather boa acts as a bridge between the world in which you are a child and the world in which you can be anyone from real life, from a film or from a story. It is the act of putting it on and talking from behind it, or through it, that does the magic of transformation for the child.

'Dressing up' is something we carry through to adult life. We are all aware that we dress in a certain way for a certain occasion, and that how we 'dress up' will affect how we feel about ourselves and how we interact with others. We are not all going to break the mould (or the internet) like Lady Gaga in her raw meat dress or David Bowie as Ziggy Stardust, but for all of us, in a sense, dressing up helps us to play a certain role. If you went to a job interview in some painting overalls, or football kit, or a wedding dress, you probably wouldn't feel that comfortable, and it wouldn't help you get into the right frame of mind, the right character, for the interview (unless it was a very specific job). This is a type of play that it can be very beneficial to continue experimenting with as an adult, changing our appearance and seeing how it enables us to inhabit different roles. I'm not suggesting you purchase a false moustache and fake glasses (although feel free to do so), but perhaps just approach your appearance in a playful manner, and see how it alters your 'character' for the day.

You won't be the only one! Cosplay (or costume play) is now a huge cultural phenomenon, and considered more performance art than simple 'dressing up'. Tens of thousands of people all over the world jump at the chance to inhabit their favourite characters, in full and often remarkably realistic outfits, at events like MCM Comic Con in London or Comiket in Tokyo. For the hardened zombies among you, you could also try Wasteland, 'the world's largest post-apocalyptic festival', in the Mojave Desert, in California, where a group of hardened survivors live and breath a heady cocktail of *Mad Max*/*Fallout*-style cosplay, heat and hard-edged music. Or you could try LARPing. Live Action Role Play (LARP) has been described as a fantasy novel, video game or the world of Dungeons and Dragons come to life. Adult players dress as their characters and enact a partly planned storyline with agreed parameters for improv and ad-libbing (there's our tool kit again!). If you've always longed for the chance to ambush your enemies in full chivalric regalia, you can – and possibly in your local woodland of a Sunday afternoon.

The End

Dramatic play, daydreaming, role-playing, theraplay (as it's been called) is a family of activities that enable us to represent the world to ourselves and to each other. It's clear from most cultures and most times that most humans of most ages do it.

When people are locked up, tightened up, holding inside them tensions, dramas, memories, traumas, then finding a way to represent them is helpful. Many people have used words like 'relief' and 'release' after this kind of pretend play or symbolic play.

It's clear that children help themselves come to terms with the complicated world they are meeting. At the heart of it is this matter of walking in other people's shoes, seeing the world from the point of view of someone else. What is more important than that? This is the basis of why and how we think, make and survive: through co-operation on the basis of each other's needs. We have to learn this stuff. If we don't, we descend into barbarism. Play is one of the great ways to practise seeing things the way others see them, if not the greatest way.

And, of course, it can be amazing fun. Almost every day, I improv some kind of situation and it feels like a tickle, a moment that breaks the routine. And that in itself is important. Routine deadens the mind and body. It is nearly always imposed on us. When we break the routine with, say, dramatic play, we take back a moment, a minute, a half-hour, in which we explore people, or ourselves, in the world for ourselves. People have said that all that we can claim for art is that, when we make it or enjoy it or think about it, we make the world at that moment bearable.

That sounds more of a downer than I intend. I mean that this stuff makes things whizzy. And who doesn't want things to be whizzy? NO ONE!

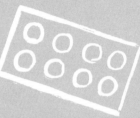

TOYS!

The Stuff of Play

We can hardly discuss play without discussing toys. For many people, the two are almost synonymous. First I want to challenge the conception of what a 'toy' is. It doesn't need to come from the supermarket or a toyshop, it doesn't need to come in plastic packaging and it doesn't need branding. Equally, it doesn't need to be an exquisitely hand-whittled spinning top or wooden train. A toy can be literally anything.

A toy is simply a physical prop that enables and enhances play. It might be a stick or a stone, an empty milk carton, a shoelace ... What makes it a toy is how we transform and use it with our imaginations. The important thing is to see the potential within an item.

Robert Louis Stevenson, a great champion of play, gives wonderful examples of this – several of his poems and one of his essays extol the joys to be had from playing with chairs, or in bed or even with porridge. In the following poem he and his companion embark on great sea voyage:

We built a ship upon the stairs
All made of the back-bedroom chairs,
And filled it full of soft pillows
To go a-sailing on the billows.

We took a saw and several nails,
And water in the nursery pails;
And Tom said, 'Let us also take
An apple and a slice of cake;' –
Which was enough for Tom and me
To go a-sailing on, till tea.

We sailed along for days and days,
And had the very best of plays;
But Tom fell out and hurt his knee,
So there was no one left but me.

(from *A Child's Garden of Verses*)

Fair enough, a few chairs and pillows have potential – and the cake speaks for itself. But how, you may well ask, does porridge, that famously dull substance, gain the elevated status of a 'toy'? Stevenson elaborates:

When my cousin and I took our porridge of a morning, we had a device to enliven the course of the meal. He ate his with sugar, and explained it to be a country continually buried under snow. I took mine with milk, and explained it to be a country suffering gradual inundation. You can imagine us exchanging bulletins; how here was an island still unsubmerged, here a valley not yet covered with snow; what inventions were made; how his population lived in cabins on perches and travelled on stilts, and how mine was always in boats; how the interest grew furious, as the last corner of safe ground was cut off on all sides and grew smaller every moment; and how in fine, the food was of altogether secondary importance, and might even have been nauseous, so long as we seasoned it with these dreams.

(from *Child's Play*)

The porridge itself might not be wildly exciting, but with a sprinkling of imagination a whole world is created.

I have often seen children playing with porridge. That claggy, lumpy beige stuff draws my mind towards water and sand. I have never been on a beach with children and not seen them dig, scoop, build walls, houses, figures, castles – usually in places where they know that the sea will wash them away. Come to that, I am rarely on a beach myself without indulging in a little sand construction work. Why do we do it? There's no point. We know that whatever we make will disappear. But we build and build, and then we stand and watch each wavelet nibbling at the structures we've made, finally overwhelming them. Sometimes we experiment by 'allowing' the sea to come under bridges and into moats and harbours. Or we might watch how it erodes the bottom of the castle walls, or make canals for it to rush further up the beach. We explore the limits of what sand can do, how it can block, control and channel. We discover the power of water on the move.

The sandcastles we build can become elaborate structures, often with several turrets and metres of walls and ramparts,

Glad Rags

Throw a party where each guest has to stick to one of the following rules at least:

- Wear only shiny things

- Dress as something dangerous

- Wear every item of clothing on the wrong part of your body

- Dress like a royal

- Everything you wear starts with the letter P (or any other letter)

- Get dressed in the dark wearing the first items you touch

- Dress like you're going on an expedition to ... Antarctica? The Amazon?

- Every item you wear has to reflect a different period in history

- Wear only items you think a robot would wear

Or make up your own rules!

perhaps a moat with a few bridges ... Have you ever tried creating an archway in a sand rampart? It's a tricky business ... Part of the joy here is not just the malleability of the material; it is the creation of this miniature world.

The Deep History of Toys

This business of building, constructing and recreating the world and ourselves in miniature has a long history. Ancient people, as far back as our cave-dwelling ancestors, made figurines that were small enough to be held in a hand. Often misleadingly we call these statuettes 'goddesses', but in fact we don't know what role they played in the lives of these ancient people. But, at the very minimum, we can see that the makers have miniaturised real-life forms, making human and animal shapes into a size that can be handled, moved and passed around, as far back as 33,000 BCE. Later on, the Ancient Egyptians made toys and games as we would understand the words today: horse-and-rider pull-alongs, animals on wheels, toy figures of cats (a sacred animal in Ancient Egypt), dolls and games involving dice, counters and squares. It is interesting to note that the same approach was taken to 'play' as to the highly ritualised and symbolic grave goods: the core idea is of transforming the world down to models that can be handled.

Of course, we have a name for miniature models of people that can be manipulated: puppets. Puppets are one of the oldest and most enduring toy forms – and also one of the most versatile:

from elaborate stringed puppets to the childhood favourite the 'sock puppet', from ventriloquist dummies to jumping jacks to finger puppets. So why are we so fascinated with puppets? Have you ever had one or taken part in a puppet show? Is it, do you think, the extraordinary way in which puppetry animates the inanimate? Is it the way dramatic play becomes amalgamated with conventional toys? And then there is the bizarre way in which children and adults will respond to a puppet as if it is a living person or animal or creature. How and why does that happen?

Puppetry has a long and celebrated history, and the puppeteers I've known feel that they are the guardians of that tradition, keeping it alive. It is full of a special language and old wrinkles to do with the craft, and to even mention this feels for a moment like giving away the tricks of the magic circle and the skill in the making and fashioning of the puppets themselves – perfecting a look around the eyes, a shape of a cheek so that as the puppet is turned there is a moment when the movement given to the puppet makes it look alive. There is something almost mystical (not quite!) in the way that audiences respond to bits of painted wood, wool, held up in front of audiences by strings, rods or with a hand. I think it is one of the most extreme examples of how willingly people of any age are prepared to withhold the 'act of comparison', to prevent themselves from making a real-life comparison between what they know the puppets are made of and the dramatic persona they watch.

Anyone say, who has watched Nina Conti with her life-size puppets or the trick she does with puppet mouths put on unsuspecting audience members will know that the craft works with adults. Then again, sitting on a beach in high summer, in the twenty-first century, it seems unbelievable that the ancient craft of Punch and Judy can work on modern children. One moment they are flicking through the files on their phones and the next they can be roaring at Mr Punch to watch out for the Crocodile – even though he's the baddie! Isn't he? And so boastful with it, prancing about on his little platform telling us all 'That's the way to do it! Clever, clever, clever Mr Punch.'

All The World's a Stage

In one way or another we can create our own puppet theatres.

The setting of the stage can be a hugely important part of play. Children often spend as long preparing the stage for their games as on the 'real' game itself, or even longer. Perhaps, in doing so, they set out the parameters for play in that particular world, placing characters or objects deliberately, unconsciously or otherwise, in order to set up potential conflict or fun and games. As we've seen, therapists like Margaret Lowenfeld suggest the setting up is just as significant as what unfolds afterwards and, from what I've seen, it can be just as fun.

Why do you think this is? Is it do with potential? After all, before the game begins, you can feel omnipotent, a creator who can visit any landscape, any time frame, any part of the universe, with any character. The bounds are those of your own imagination.

I've always been rather fond of what are known as Pollock's Paper Theatres ('Penny plain, Tuppence coloured', as the Victorian advertisement put it). You construct the little theatre and the characters from the plays by cutting out the parts, which are printed on card, and sticking it all together. The little theatres are true miniature gems, ornate and sumptuous, with their regal red curtains (paper), gold brocade (paper) and the elaborately painted proscenium arch (also paper). The printed characters are frozen in time, with a Victorian postcard look about them which defies their sometimes grandiose characters. In my eagerness to get my children to play with the paper theatres, I cut it all out, stuck it together, mounted the characters on the rods and even rewrote the plays that were provided by the makers! We did put on a show or two, but I fear I was much too bossy for it to really stick as something that the children wanted to do for themselves.

This is itself is interesting. While my children appreciated my enthusiasm and input, ultimately they didn't want to be told what to do. This taught me a lesson: it is great for adults to get involved in children's games – but usually (I say with regret) it is not applicable to play. In fact, studies show that children don't regard this kind of 'organised fun' as genuine play at all. Play is an opportunity for children to own the freedom, for them to assume authority and control over the world that they have created – after all, so often the world is controlled for them, without them having much say in the matter.

Bought, commercial or home-made stage sets vary hugely in the level of realism with which they depict the world. Some children prefer the toy buildings that 'look real', just like the

Ice Block Skyscraper

Take some ice cubes and stack them on top of one another to create a frozen skyscraper (remember to protect your floor). How tall can your building get before it topples over? If you feel like being competitive play with a friend.

19
18
17
16
15
14
13
12
11
10
9
8
7
6
5
4
3
2
1

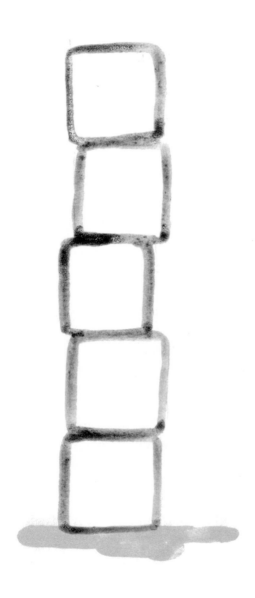

real world, but tiny. Other children are perfectly happy to construct a building out of a cardboard box with windows they cut into it. For some, the stage is no more than a symbol of the landscape they have created in their mind, whereas for others part of the joy in the construction is making it as realistic as possible. There is no judgement as to which is a superior or more beneficial way of playing; they are simply different approaches. These different approaches may well continue into adulthood. Are you someone who wants to reflect reality as closely as possible? Or are you more broad-brushstroke, more symbolic? If I asked you to draw me a cat, would you try and make it look as lifelike as possible, like you could hear it purr? Or would you be happier giving the impression of a cat, trying to capture its essence, its 'cattishness'? Whichever camp you fall into, it's interesting to try putting yourself in the other for a day – if you're a realist, you can try approaching things symbolically, and vice versa.

My daughter was hooked for a while on Playmobil. Here you have rather unrealistic figures, looking a bit like plastic versions of the old peg-dolls which I remember from the 1950s. In contrast, the 'sets' are very realistic. She and her best friend loved to 'animate' the little figures in their primary-coloured tops and hats, as they went to the stables or to their favourite, the hospital (sometimes as a result of having visited the stables). A good deal of time involved starting from scratch each time, putting the 'set' together, before they started moving the ambulances, summoning doctors, nurses and hospital workers, mending legs and saving lives. Sometimes she helped her younger brother set up the airport, and they played landing and taking off, and averting major disasters. There was also an ice-cream parlour, where she and her friend served and 'ate' endless combinations of flavours and toppings.

Toys as Tools

So, the act of constructing the set for the intended 'play' can often be as much a part of play as the eventual narrative. In the case of construction toys such as Lego and Duplo, the figurines are secondary to the act of building, the principle on which Lego was founded.

Over two millennia ago, the idea that construction and play were intertwined was already recognised. The fourth-century BCE philosopher Plato believed that play was an essential grounding for the architects and builders of the future. He is cited as saying, 'the future builder must play at building [...] and those who have care of their education should provide them, when young, with mimic tools' (quoted in *Children's Spaces*, edited by Mark Dudek). This is one of the earliest examples we have of the school of thought that playing in certain ways is educational. It's the argument which says that the business of miniaturising reality enables a person to try things out, to bring into being things that one might first imagine and to carry out some kind of test to see whether such once imagined things work.

Perhaps Plato had in mind the models that children and adults made in his time of boats, harbours and temples. In essence,

NICE THROW

Try throwing a teabag into a cup from as far away as possible. First to hit the target wins.

Too easy? Throw a slice of bread into the toaster from as far away as you can – right into the slot.

creating a prototype for the real world. As we discussed with dramatic play, it is a low-risk, no-consequence place of safety in which to experiment with the world, its opportunities and its limitations.

Certainly, history is full of people who played as children and carried that inquisitiveness and curiosity with them into adulthood. Leonardo da Vinci, for example, played and kept on playing with different materials and skills. The biographer Giorgio Vasari, writing shortly after Leonardo's death, reports that he threw himself headlong into everything he did as a child. He 'never ceased drawing', outsmarted his maths tutor within a few months and mastered the lyre. 'He sang divinely to that instrument,' reports Vasari, and enjoyed 'improvising upon it'. Leonardo struggled to finish work as a child, and in later life, but he was always playing and branching out: painting, anatomical studies, designing weapons and bridges. Famously, of course, he even designed a prototype helicopter, more than four hundred years before the first one took flight.

This is not to say that if you give your child a pack of pencils and a lyre, they'll one day paint the *Mona Lisa*. Freedom in play and the chance to explore do, however, often foster a lifetime of creativity. Tim Berners-Lee, inventor of the World Wide Web, was a keen young trainspotter and taught himself all about electronics by fiddling with his model railway. He carried that playful curiosity forward to university, where he built a computer using an old TV and a soldering iron. Likewise, consider Grace Hopper, a rear-admiral in the US Navy and a pioneering computer scientist, known as the 'Queen of Code'. She started disassembling and rebuilding alarm clocks as a child, and later became the third person ever to programme Harvard's early Mark I computer. She won numerous awards in her lifetime, including the inaugural Computer Science Man (!) of the Year Award in 1969, which is rather telling, isn't it? Someone else who tinkered and played throughout her life was Hedy Lamarr, better known in her lifetime as a Hollywood actress but also a prolific inventor. She used to carry out experiments in her trailer during breaks from filming, and in 1942 patented a frequency-hopping idea that eventually led to the development of Wi-Fi technology.

Putting any expectation on play and experimental activity may rather suck the joy out of it, but as psychiatrist Dr Stuart Brown argues, it's well worth examining what he calls your unique 'play history', looking for those moments that excited you most as a child, that gave you pure delight. He suggests they are the key to identifying our true passions and inner drive. Worth a try, isn't it? Why not jot down in the margin here a moment of play that gave you an intense feeling of pleasure?

Toys designed to nurture this kind of inventiveness in children have a long history. In his *Some Thoughts Concerning Education* (1693), the philosopher John Locke was perhaps the first to write about putting letters on dice. These became known as 'Locke's blocks'. Children could learn their alphabet while playing, and presumably at the same time build some very impressive towers. Later, in the eighteenth century, Maria and Richard Lovell Edgeworth also advocated giving infants 'pieces of wood of various shapes and sizes, which they may build up and pull down'. They suggested that older children experiment with blocks of wood and stones, so that they could learn, through experience, the basic principles of physics (*Practical Education*, 1798). But it's arguable that blocks really hit the big time thanks to Friedrich Fröbel, the founder of the first kindergarten in nineteenth-century Germany, who remains hugely influential to this day. He made blocks a fundamental component of his 'gifts', a set of specially constructed objects, designed to encourage open-ended play. Between then and my own childhood many different kinds of construction toys were produced, my brother's favourite being Meccano and mine Brickplayer.

Meccano began life in 1898 in Liverpool, the invention of Frank Hornby. It was a system of perforated metal strips, plates, girders, wheels, axles and gears, all of which were held together by nuts and bolts. As a system you could make very simple shapes or huge complex moving machines – a Ferris wheel, a retracting bridge, a helicopter with rotating blades. Anything you constructed had the look of an iron girder bridge, with its nuts and bolts visible to the eye. This meant that when you were constructing something industrial or mechanical, it achieved one of the aims that miniaturising celebrates – realism. 'That looks so realistic,' my brother and I would say with pleasure. The moment you made things like houses or animals, the effect wasn't so good. Clearly, we weren't so into symbolic play that we could tolerate nuts and bolts sticking out of the side of a Meccano-built horse. As Plato and the Edgeworths anticipated, the process was full of cognitive learning: how tight do you tighten a nut? How do you construct things so that they don't fall down? And how do gears work? What combination of cogs makes a wheel go round faster – small to big? Big to small? To the amazement of our parents, my brother spent several days, possibly weeks, constructing a 'universal joint', a quite complex mechanism that allows the arms to rotate at any given angle. I imagine many adults would struggle to construct one of these, certainly without the aid of the internet to guide them! Go on, I challenge you.

I preferred another kind of realism, as I saw it at the time: Brickplayer. This began life in 1938, invented by the board game company J. W. Spear. As the witty title suggests, you 'played' and 'laid' very small red bricks, sticking them together with a 'mortar' made from flour and chalk powder to build scale models of buildings according to what were, in effect, architect's plans. These could take a week or more to make. To reuse the bricks, you had to soak the whole construction in water, loosening the mortar until the whole building fell apart. So not exactly durable in the 'real' world. But this was Plato in action! I was of course making a version of a doll's house – but the gender-defined play that was par for the course back then in the 1950s was blurred with Brickplayer – it may have been a doll's house but it was also construction, a typically 'masculine' role. I can say now that I experienced the full joy of the 'realistic' aspect that comes with miniaturisation. My greatest pleasure was putting my finished buildings onto a large green piece of felt, getting out sets of model animals and 'playing farms'. As with our ancient cave-dwelling ancestors, this was a way of bringing the world (as I knew it from camping holidays) into our home. By making that world smaller, I could bring it from 'out there' to 'in here' and manage it. I would move my farmer around, going from barn to house to field to pond. I milked cows, collected eggs. Horses galloped and ducks quacked. I controlled the world.

Not Paper Aeroplanes

Make a paper aeroplane ... out of anything other than paper!

You can use anything else, but it must still be vaguely aeroplane-shaped.

Hint: Alternative materials might include a dishcloth – if you wet it and freeze it, it will be more aerodynamic – or a sponge, a cereal box ...

This idea, that by making things small we control them, sometimes grips adults. H. G. Wells, who wrote among other things that great toy-giant fantasy *The War of the Worlds* (1897), also wrote the little-known book *Little Wars* (1913). Whereas my brother and I stopped playing toy soldiers when we 'grew out of it' – a curious phrase that we should question more – Wells as an adult created these elaborate outdoor toy soldier games, full of rules of engagement, battle, surrender and the rest, and laid them out in all seriousness in this book, full of maps, diagrams, illustrations and photos. It's only at the end, when we may wonder whether the whole book is itself some kind of satire, that he writes:

> You only have to play at Little Wars three or four times to realize just what a blundering thing Great War must be [...] Not only are the masses of men and material and suffering and inconvenience too monstrously big for reason, but – the available heads we have for it, are too small.

As a child, I got a glimpse of what happens when adults play with the world of miniatures and the possibilities inherent with a little more life experience and, quite probably, superior tools and materials. On a couple of occasions we visited Bekonscot, a miniature village near Beaconsfield in Buckinghamshire. This was first created in the 1920s by Roland Callingham. You can wander in and out of the knee-high buildings and experience a similar kind of temporary omnipotence, even though you haven't made the models and you can't move the trains and boats yourself. My memory of this is that it was both supremely wonderful and magical but at the same time slightly inhibiting. I would never be able to make something so good, so special, so exciting. My creations seemed limited in comparison. The last straw for me was walking downstairs with my large Brickplayer farmhouse across my forearms, when it broke in half and fell into many pieces all over the stairs. Perhaps I should have realised that the chalk-flour mortar was not strong enough, perhaps I should have given it a more secure foundation and brought it downstairs on a tray, but I was young and learning through my early mistakes. Sadly, my overriding sense on viewing the shattered remains of my farmhouse was that I wasn't up to the task, my construction and building management were not good enough. This unfortunately ended with me putting my Brickplayer to one side. (I still have the animals, though, to this day.)

This kind of frustration can be productive. I think I've heard all my children and stepchildren – girls and boys – at some point or another weeping with annoyance at Lego as an arch caves in, a wheel falls off or it simply doesn't look like it did in their head. Part of constructing small things out of units is confronting the limitations of materials. Plastic is plastic, wood is wood, metal is metal. When we play with these materials, we discover what they can and can't do. It may seem obvious to us as adults, but part of play is about learning which materials bend, which don't, which materials can fit and lock into each other, which can't. Play is a perfect way to discover these things.

It is also about discovering your limits as architect and – and this is crucial – watching those limitations diminish as you become more proficient in your design and construction. When this is scaled up, when the child of today becomes the architect of tomorrow, amazing feats of engineering can take

FOODSCAPES

Make a mythical landscape out of your dinner. Broccoli
as trees or potatoes as rocks. Cauliflower clouds?
Spinach forest? What is the ketchup going to represent?
Aaaaarrrrgggh!!!

If you want to really challenge yourself, try and make a scene
from a film. How about *The Wizard of Oz*, with a yellow
brick road made of sweetcorn?

place. Having experimented with the limits of string and wire in building a bridge to span the kitchen table, it is in some ways just a matter of scaling up – in thoughts, material, ambition – until you get the Akashi Kaikyō Bridge, the longest suspension bridge in the world, whose steel cables are long enough to circle the earth over seven times.

The Commodification of Play

Sometimes, as a parent, or just as a critically minded human being, you can feel as if you are caught in a web of consumerism. From this position, it is difficult to define oneself outside of the web. Happiness is a Barbie. Happiness is a Tonka Truck. As an adult, we simply up the price tag on happiness – happiness is a new car, a new phone, a fancier holiday. The message we are bombarded with is the need for gratification: that you, as a child, cannot be happy unless you have the toy you've seen at your friend's house, in an ad on TV, online or in a shop window. As an adult, the message changes subtly – you cannot be successful or fulfilled, you cannot be living life to the full, unless you have this phone, this car, go on this holiday ... We are what we buy ... Yum yum, say the manufacturers.

As we move along the aisles of the toyshops or surf the endless labyrinthine supermarket of the internet, we may wonder whether what matters most in this process is not whether our children play in the most imaginative ways but in what way they become consumers of the future. Toys are, after all, our first steps into this consumer-driven culture. This moment was captured in the most satirical and ironic way possible in *Toy Story 2,* when Buzz Lightyear sees a shop selling Buzz Lightyears and he is full of awe at the sight. For a moment, we as viewers might forget that 'he' doesn't exist! 'He' is an image created from inside the greatest industry of mechanical reproduction ever invented, the Walt Disney Company. Does this mass production decrease the value of the toy? Does it lose its individual potential? Or does it teach us a valuable lesson about how we can take something that is not unique and make it individual? Not long after the film came out I went into a toyshop, and of course there were Buzz Lightyears by the score on the shelves – and I bought one for my kids. At this point I think I got lost in whether I was laughing or whether the last laugh was on me.

It is easy to reminisce about the toys of our own childhoods, and see them through a nostalgic, rose-tinted haze. But was Buzz so very different from Meccano, Brickplayer or indeed the huge effort and expenditure that went into the train sets that my brother, our friends and I collected? Was this different from the Barbie Dolls, Sylvanian Families, Playmobil and Lego figures that my children have played with?

The prevalence of 'merchandise' toys has by no means done away with their counterpart – non-commercial or hand-crafted toys. The huge success of sites like Etsy shows a growing market for toys that are hand-produced, unique, individual (or nearly so) or even flawed. There are, and I would cautiously state always will be, a whole world of toys made by parents, relatives or friends – or by the child themselves. It can be a

Newspaper Headgear

You don't need to be able to sew to make your own hat!
Use old newspaper, masking tape and scissors instead.

Do you fancy a Chef's Hat, Princess Tiara, Queen's Crown,
Witch's Hat or Astronaut's Helmet?

beautiful thing and an act of love, in which a child sees a parent devoting hours of effort and skill entirely to them.

HIS & HERS: The Gendering of Toys

Mass-produced or commercial toys are not new. Even in Stevenson's day, while he was happily playing with his porridge, and before, there were toys available in shops to be bought by those who could afford them, and there was of course a living to be made in making them. The toy industry is now a huge worldwide business and is part of how we are defined as consumers. A triangle is formed between the toy, the buyer and the child, and within this we have choices to make. This little triangle is one in which we make statements about what we think about childhood, gender, play, consumption, design and much more. Short of not buying any toys ever, as adults we end up buying toys that go towards defining the child. The overwhelming narrative in this has historically been that toys define girls as cooks, clothes wearers and 'princesses', and boys as adventurers, scientists and killers. While this narrative is changing, it may still at times feel inescapable. Even if we consciously don't buy into it, there's every chance that someone we know does, whether it's our children's grandparents, their best friend's parents, their aunts or uncles.

Gender roles and how they have infiltrated the world of childhood and play go back millennia. In earlier times, humans created rites for young men to prove themselves for their later roles as hunters and warriors. On a personal level, you might argue that I created one of these for myself when I played at being an astronaut in the coal bunker as a child. It was, of course, just possible that I might one day have become a military pilot, or indeed an astronaut, but it was far more likely that I would stereotypically live my life in a role in which I would be expected to cope, manage, lead, take risks, be adventurous, have people rely on me, grit my teeth, not collapse under the strain of difficulty, not allow myself to be too emotional when awful things happened around me and so on. This is part of the way in which masculinity is 'taught' through play. Of course, a parallel set of expectations exists for girls and the kinds of roles being imagined for them. The market for dolls and toy cookery sets is still predominantly aimed at young girls.

I suspect that at an early stage in my life I was aware of the stories and symbols around me that were suggesting what I should be doing later in life. One way I could 'try out' the roles that were 'beckoning me' was to play them out in the coal bunker, or to play with the toy soldiers or trucks that I was given. I've watched two stepdaughters and one daughter of my own doing their role-plays and have seen how they have done equivalent role-playing from within the stereotypes that surrounded them. They played out being supercooks, nurses, nursery school teachers and, of course, mothers, over and over again. I've also seen them enthusiastically trying out the role of singer soloist and dancer, working out routines, poses, acting crises – the full showbiz works. Some might see these as evidence of how my children were acting from exposure to conditioning. I concede that this is part of the story. I also think that it's not the whole story. The bigger picture of what's

Making in Miniature

Make tiny versions of things that are normally big.

MAKE A TINY ...

- crown
- boat (it must float)
- windmill (with moving sails)
- animal
- scarecrow
- castle
- spaceship
- Eiffel Tower

OUT OF ...

- paper (any sort – newspaper, loo roll, kitchen towel)
- soap
- cheese
- pegs
- an apple
- a flowerpot
- pasta
- an empty jar/bottle
- bottle tops
- corks (real or plastic)

Hint: You'll need a store of 'essentials' –
Sellotape, Blu Tack, string, cocktail sticks, scissors
etc. – in addition to your sculpting material.

going on is that these gendered roles are full of expectations that are greater than we are. In other words, we can never be as good in real life as the ideal images of men and women we are shown on TV and films – and in our toys. Boys have to live up to their superhero action figures and save the world; girls have to dress their dolls perfectly and show maternal instincts at a ludicrously young age. At some level this gives us anxieties: what if I'm not (in my case) a superhero, a superpilot; in the case of girls, a supermum or a supercook or a supersinger? One way to play with that anxiety is indeed to play it out. Note, I don't say 'resolve' it. Perhaps we never do that! But until the toy market reflects total gender neutrality, can we ever erase this conditioning?

The very shape of play, the kinds of toys we play with, can not only be heavily gendered but also heavily loaded towards 'types' which show and reflect 'dominant' ideas about what is or is not an ideal person, often failing to reflect many in terms of race, class or disability.

Here's a game you can play in a group situation: bring in a variety of toys, cuddly toy animals and creatures, dolls and 'action' figures – superheroes and the like. Make sure that there is the widest possible variety. Put them on a table where everyone can see them and talk! Invite people to talk about the toys they had, that they wished they had, that they saw other people had. Invite them to talk about what they think of these toys and dolls and figures. What expectations come with them, do you think? Would they have wanted any of these – why, or why not? What kinds of figure are not represented in this selection? Does that matter? What kinds of figures can people make themselves? Is that important?

The Secret Life of Toys

It should be said at this point that toys are not just building blocks with which to play out the real world. Nor are they merely the beginning of a lifetime of gender conditioning, or of consumerism. They are, one could say first and foremost, repositories of an overpowering desire in children to believe in a secret other world, an almost mystical world that they know is there and can somehow access through toys. In the hands of the player toys are (or become) magical. You've seen small children play with their toys, talk to them and, crucially, listen to what they say in response. For children, their toys are living entities.

Anyone who is a parent or a teacher of young children will have observed the way children will talk to their soft toys, or make their soft toys 'talk' to them. They often create dramatic situations for the soft toys to take part in, based on the child's experience of real life: teatime, going to the doctor's, going to play group, going on holiday, going on journeys. Replicas of TV and film characters, dolls and a host of other toy heroes and animals can be recruited for these games, where the dramas that they appear in on-screen can be reinvented, recycled or mixed up. Often children have no problem with mixing up

Stop Frame

Most phones and tablets let you create stop-frame animations.

Use paper, felt-tips, fruit, kitchen utensils or whatever you can find around the house to tell a fifteen- to thirty-second stop-frame animation.

Hint: To save time you can do the commentary or the voices 'live' when you show it.

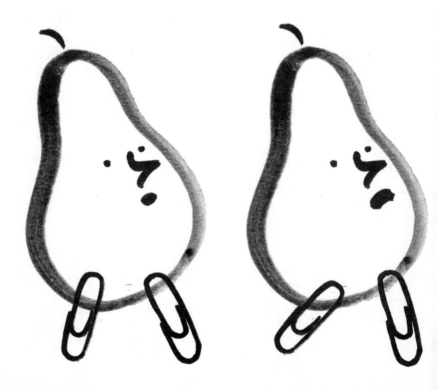

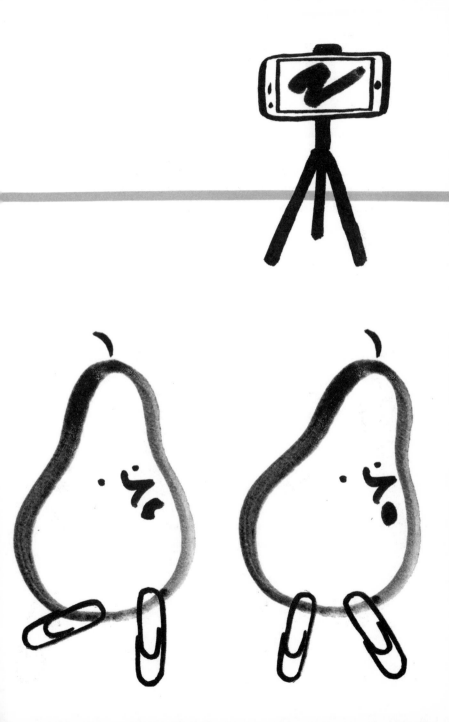

the toys: a Superman figure with a teddy bear, or a doll with a plastic bear. Toys in this sense, then, are limitless and do not have to be constrained by the categories of the 'real world'.

The belief that the toy is in some way 'alive' is so strong that it gave rise to one of the most popular film franchises of recent decades, touched on above: *Toy Story*. These films resonate with young and old alike because they tap into something that we secretly all believe, or once believed: that our toys are living their own secret existence. Toys give shape to our fundamental desire to believe that the world is bigger and more magical and mysterious than the day-to-day that we see around us.

Eventually, however, many toys get 'used up' and children grow bored of them or 'outgrow them' – as in *Toy Story 2*. Is this indicative of a running out of imagination? Or is it simply a natural desire to move on, discover new things, push new boundaries?

Even with the most inert and unchangeable toys, if a toy or object is played with again and again, the game being played out won't be exactly the same. The toy comes into the next play with some of the animation it acquired during the previous play, or any of the previous plays. Part of the fun of a good play is the continuity and variation involved: using the familiarity but working in some variations this time round. And the time after. And that's how toys that seem undamaged and, as adults often think, still in good condition come to be 'used up'. From the child's point of view there are no more variations to play. There's no more novelty you can introduce.

The Digital Playground

The ultimate modern toy, or rather modern playground, for millions of children, teenagers and adults is in the digital world. Please let me be clear from the start: I have spent hours and hours in this place – playing Sonic the Hedgehog, Super Mario, Tekken, SimCity and even trying to play the football games, the various incarnations of FIFA. I've had great times larking about, arguing, joking while playing these. Yes, they are play but they are, I would argue, quite heavily 'rule-bound'. That's part of the fun, of course: you operate within or against what is set; your range of options is limited. But, as you will have noticed, this book is mostly about the kind of play that either has no rules or only a few rules, or where part of the play is that you set the rules. The trial-and-error bit, I think, is crucial because this is what allows us to experiment. Tell me otherwise – shout at me, if you like – but I've found these games too limiting on the trial-and-error front. Perhaps you've found ways to open them up.

But then again, these kinds of games are far, far from everything you can play in the digital world. There is an immense range of apps and systems that allow you to make animations, play with photos, videos and graphics of all kind. I have one reason to know about this only too well. My son makes videos of me performing my poems. Hey, while we're on that, why don't you do that? My son put them up on YouTube, then other people who roam the internet looking for material they can use to do 'mash-ups', or what they call 'poops', found me. And they started

Giant Cardboard Fort

Draw up some architectural plans, then rummage in the recycling bin to find cardboard boxes of all shapes and sizes.

Clear a space in your living room or outside and use scissors, tape and anything else you find lying around to make your fort in thirty minutes. The tallest fort (that doesn't collapse) wins!

clipping it, doing montages of me, doing weird distortions of my face, chopping up the things I say and so on. To start with, I was cross – I thought they were 'stealing' my work. Then they pointed out that 'If you put stuff on YouTube, you must expect that people will play with it!' What does this tell me? It tells me that there are many parts of the digital world that have really become new play spaces. There are editing apps which allow people of almost any age to play with sound, graphics and moving images, doing that early twentieth-century thing of cut-outs, clips, distortions, animations and the rest. It reminds me that whenever there are technological changes, people will get among them, play with them and produce outcomes that weren't expected in the first place. Travel to Paris and you end up staring at a perfect example of this: the French engineers, particularly Monsieur Eiffel, said to themselves, if we can make cast-iron cheaply enough and bolt it together strongly enough, what could we build? Ho hum ... ermm ... what about a really, really tall tower? Let's do it! And they did. Voilà la Tour Eiffel!

So the rule is – when we change the technology, we change the play space. We change the materials and we change where it is. And what does that mean, when we're talking about the digital playground? It does mean that the person playing there may well not move from their chair for hours on end. Does that matter? You tell me!

Playful Learning

To Play is to Learn

We have seen many examples throughout the previous five chapters of how play can enhance our experience of the world, introduce us to new experiences, improve the way we interact with people and help us handle things that worry or frighten us. But as soon we start to introduce terms like education, knowledge, teaching, learning-through-play, discovery-learning and the like, and discuss them in conjunction with the word 'play', we often do two things that are not always very helpful: we tend to think of such ideas as being very one-dimensional, as if they each consist of one process; and then, because they are separate words, we tend to think of them each as separate processes, sealed off from each other. Easily done!

Let me illustrate the kind of confusion this leads us into. My father was first a teacher and then a teacher-trainer who supervised teachers in training. He would go into schools and watch his students making their first steps in teaching. In the evenings he would often tell us stories of what he had seen and heard. One time he told us that he was sitting in the staff room when a teacher walked in and called out to her colleagues, 'Well, I've taught it to them. Whether they've learned it or not, is a different matter.' Then, straight after he told me that, he fell about laughing.

I was about seventeen years old at the time. What was funny about it? I thought, isn't that what goes on in schools? Teachers stand out the front, they teach and some of us 'get' it and some of us don't. If the teacher 'gets through' the course, then they've done their bit. Surely it's our problem if we haven't learned it? My father tried to explain that 'teaching' has to include 'learning'; otherwise there's no point to teaching. He was trying to get me to see that these two separate words aren't as clearly separated off from each other as we often think they are. (Interesting, isn't it, that my dad used to explain difficult ideas like this with a story. In a way that's quite playful.) I tell this story too, as a warning to myself that, the moment we get too 'mechanical' about words and their meanings, we might end up distorting what really goes on. This is particularly important when we talk about play, play and learning, play in education. Simply by using the word 'play', we often make it seem less important than, say, education, work, knowledge or 'real' learning – whatever that is. After all, the word 'play' has emotional and historical links to words like 'idleness', 'escapism', 'frivolity', 'leisure' and various kinds of 'pointlessness'. Education, learning and knowledge, on the other hand, are (we often tell ourselves) serious and important, and they are what will get us jobs, status and high earnings. However, as we've seen through the course of this book, it's not as simple as that – play is fundamental to our development as people and, more broadly, as a society and culture. It's a mistake to think of all play and education in watertight compartments, separated off from each other.

Let's have a go, then, at some key ideas and definitions that will help us round these ideas. First: what we do we mean by knowledge – a word more often associated with education than with play? Sometimes we think of knowledge as 'general knowledge', the stuff that wins you the pub quiz or gets you good marks in school, and so it's easy to assume that, the more of this 'knowledge' you have, the brainier and more successful you must be. This is certainly what underpins TV programmes like *University Challenge* and *Mastermind*. Knowledge contains the word 'know'. In general speech, it's interesting to notice that we use the word 'knowing' in quite a few different ways. Some languages have different words to describe different kinds of knowledge: both French and German have a word for knowing a person or place (connaître and kennen), and another word for knowing 'stuff' like maths (savoir and wissen). Then there are associated phrases for knowing how to do something – one of which we've borrowed from French: savoir faire, which we use to mean the ability to act or speak appropriately or which can just mean being cool and suave in the kind of situation that others find tricky. We also have a sense that knowledge is a very broad term, and that it can encompass things we might express at other times as 'know-how', 'common sense' or 'nous' (a word I enjoy using, by the way!). In this sense, the word 'knowledge' clumps together a range of skills, abilities and ways of doing things that we remember, and we learn a lot of these things not through education but, I would argue, through forms of play.

Conduct your own science experiment

Bear in mind those four principles we explored: investigate, interpret, invent, co-operate. Now come up with your own experiment or investigation: it might be scientific, artistic, musical or academic. Perhaps there's a subject that's always interested you and you want to find out more?

Try thinking about some of the following challenges:

- Can you make a model volcano that erupts?

- Can you make a rainbow?

- Can you make a raw egg bounce?

DO AS YOU'RE TOLD (OR NOT...)

As Albert Einstein said, 'Anyone who has never made a mistake has never tried anything new.'

One of the best and most useful ways we learn is from our mistakes. But, naturally, we all try and avoid making them – sometimes we try so hard not to make a mistake that we don't even try.

Are we too reliant on instructions these days? Everything comes with a manual. And even if it doesn't, there's always the internet. So try to complete these tasks – *without looking up any instructions.* When mistakes happen – learn from them, adjust, and try again!

- Bake some cookies.

- Make papier mâché.

- Make a jelly from scratch.

- Sew a cushion cover.

- Make a paper 'fortune-teller'.

We also use the word 'know' when we say, 'she knows how to ...' do such things as walk or talk or run. (How did we get to 'know' these things?) We also learn more abstract skills from a young age, such as how to watch moving images (TV and film) or how to mix with other people ('socialisation'), in many, many different ways. These are not frivolous things. They are right at the heart of how we live and who we are. But how do we get this knowledge? Well, this is very interesting, because we mostly get the hang of these things without someone else instructing us. Take that in for a moment. Usually, the moment we think of 'learning' we link that to someone 'teaching' us. I often say to my wife that I would like to be better at French. We then go into a chat about what kind of class or what kind of teacher I might need. That's the mindset. But when it comes to walking and talking and running about, we don't usually think of these as needing a teacher – unless therapy or sports coaching is involved. The significance of this remarkable fact is that we can say that most of us have the potential to learn knowledge – at least, the kind of knowledge involved in walking and talking (and other processes too?) through some kind of combination of copying, practising and learning from what we might think of as 'mistakes' or 'not getting it right first time' – which I would call 'play'. Again, think about this for a moment. It means that there is a powerful ability to learn inside us. Think on: at times, as we're learning how to walk and talk (or some other things you might think of right now), other people might suggest to us that we're getting something wrong, but if they overdo this, it may not be helpful or it may even put us off. Many of us are very tender souls. We get put off learning very easily. (That's me and musical instruments and maths!) I used the word 'practising' earlier, but this may give the wrong impression, as we often think of practising as repeating something like an exercise on the piano or learning how to get a choreographed dance routine. When we learn the piano or dance, we practise something very specific, over and over again, till we get it right. In the little list of examples I gave (walking, talking, running) I mean a practice that is more tentative than that, more 'suck-it-and-see', more trial-and-error – that is: play!

So, I've done a little dance around and through 'knowledge' and 'know' and a bit on 'learning'. I hope you might now be thinking that these words are bit trickier, a bit messier, a bit fuzzier than the kind of definitions we get in a dictionary. Perhaps you can make it even fuzzier by thinking of some other odd or surprising ways in which we use knowledge, apart from the more obvious ones of knowledge of how to do trigonometry, or knowing the names of the muscles in our neck or what Aristotle wrote about tragedy. If we want to think about play and learning, we'll need a good, 3D, fuzzy idea of what knowledge and knowing and getting-to-know can mean. 'Hey, and don't give me that knowing smile!' Think about that: how do we know how to be knowing?

Now let's move on to education.

Education, like knowledge, also defies a simple definition. On the one hand, education seems to suggest in our mind that teachers are involved. So is education the act of someone helping us acquire knowledge? Often, yes. But it can also refer to an enlightening experience that provides us with knowledge without active teaching from a third party. Can you think of moments like this that were an 'education' to you? When I was seventeen, I was knocked down in the road and had to spend about eight weeks in hospital and another two in a rehabilitation centre, where I had to teach myself how to walk! I had lost the knowledge of how to do that. The whole experience was an 'education' for me because of the other people in the ward, the nurses, the orderlies and the doctors – an amazing, diverse cross-section of people all with stories to tell, along with a lot of banter, teasing, joke-telling, that we might put into the category of being playful, or indeed full-on play. So, while knowledge and education are linked, it is not as simple as education = knowledge. Play can provide an enlightening experience (which sometimes we do call 'education'), and this brings with it new knowledge.

Is all this getting complicated? I hope so. As you read, you might like to think of these words and ideas as juggling balls. You might like to interrupt the flow of what I have written with questions like 'What about ...? ' or 'What if ...?' You don't have to just 'take' what I'm saying. You can play with it. That way, I promise you, my ideas and your ideas will create new shapes, new or altered 'constructs' (as some people call them) in your mind.

Baby Talk

Let's go back to learning to talk. In my time I've watched seven children grow from not being able to talk to being fluent talkers. This is an amazing, stupendous, incredible and wonderful thing. Because it is so common and usual, it's easy to overlook just how amazing it is. Language is a stunningly complex, varied matter. Linguists have spent hundreds of years trying to describe it, how it works, how it changes and where it comes from – and they're still arguing about it, and yet we get most of its principles and structures when we are at our least mature, least able to understand concepts and emotions, least able to understand how the world works, and when we are at our most vulnerable, most feeble, most in need of help for survival. It's the time when we think of humans as being 'little', and many people talk of babies and toddlers as having 'little minds': I've heard many people say, 'I wonder what's going on in his little mind.' And yet we do this incredibly sophisticated, complex thing of acquiring the knowledge of how to use language. Come on, it's a wonder, isn't it?

People have researched this process of language acquisition, as it's called, and written many books about it, but there is nothing to match the incredible joy of hearing this happen for yourself. If you can, just tune in to the hundreds or thousands of different ways in which toddlers play with the sounds, structures, words and grammar of language. At its most intense, between roughly the ages of one and four, it is extreme play, a full-on all-day, experimental, trial-and-error, suck-it-and-see activity. And language is a skill-and-knowledge-in-one thing. And mostly it's not exactly taught in the usual sense. It is encouraged and developed by parents and other adults, often in playful ways through songs, rhymes, games or just by hanging out and talking!

In some ways, small babies are a bit like animals, in that their needs are pretty basic – food and comfort. Interestingly, they can't convey these needs through words. Yet right from the start they're very good at communicating their needs about food and comfort without spoken language. They do it by using their faces, hands, whole bodies and, of course, their voices. In response to these 'signs' (a word we can use for this kind of pre-language communication), more often than not, we talk to them, at them and about them. Some of this is seemingly pointless. I can't think of the hundreds of times I've said things like, 'And how are you today, miss?' and 'What's up?' and 'Here comes the spoon' to pre-spoken language-speaking babies. Or I have sung songs like 'We All Live in a Yellow Submarine', played interactive games with them ('action rhymes') like 'Round and Round the Garden' ... If we're doing all this when the baby is, let's say, three months old, the baby won't be speaking back to us with words. They may well respond with what we think and hope are satisfied or joyful little noises and facial expressions, but they're not fully fledged words. But there's an enormous amount of knowledge going in and being processed by babies' incredible minds.

Pause for a moment – remember there is something very absurd about language. There really is no rational reason why the sounds 't' 'ay' 'b' and a kind of 'ull' sound should signify a table. There is nothing table-y about the word 'table'. There is nothing about most of the words we use that is connected to their meaning. (Mind you, some words are connected – think 'quack' and 'clap' and 'croak'. And what about all those 'sl' words that seem to be about things being slippery, slidey, sloshy, slappy, sloppy ...?) Even more complicated: is there a reason why a statement has an order of words for 'You are big' but when we ask a question, it has a word order of 'Are you big?' Is there anything questiony about turning things round? Is there anything very 'now' about putting '-ing' on the end of some words? Is there anything very 'in the past' about putting '-ed' on the ends of some words? What I'm saying here is that much of this stuff is very, very mysterious, complicated and without logical reason. And yet we learn it and know how this stuff works pretty well signed, sealed and done by the time we're four or five – apart from adding a bit of complexity in structure and of course 'vocabulary' or new words. The basic and amazing principles, though, we've got hold of, most of it through imitation and play.

Whether our talk is while we 'work' (feeding, dressing, cleaning the baby or getting it to sleep) or what we think of as play (singing, joking), everything we know about how we learn to talk tells us that the baby is processing what we say and how we say it, and they are inferring and deducing meaning from it, mostly from the contexts of gesture, facial expression and 'consequence'. If I say 'x', 'y' happens. If you say 'z', 'a' happens – and the millions of variations on that. Babies are then 'transmitting' back to us, observing the effects of what they have transmitted and, in turn, responding to those effects. And, as anyone who has watched babies knows, they also sit on their own playing with – at the very least – the apparatus we are born with for making sounds: diaphragm, lungs, larynx, vocal cords, tongue, teeth, lips. At least some of this is connected to sucking, chewing, swallowing and sticking fingers in their mouths.

Rainforest in a bottle

Why not bring a bit of nature indoors?
Build your very own tiny rainforest.

You will need:

- a large plastic bottle or clear jar that you can seal;

- some flower seeds and some moss;

- a cup full of soil;

- half a cup of gravel or small stones.

To construct your rainforest:

- cut the bottle in half;

- sprinkle some gravel in the bottom (this will act as drainage);

- sprinkle the soil on top and plant your seeds in it;

- top this with a layer of moss;

- water it;

- cut a slit in the top half of the bottle so that you can squeeze it back over the bottom half, and seal with Sellotape.

Voila! A rainforest in a bottle – it creates its own tiny ecosystem, so you won't even have to water it.

Let's look a bit more closely at some of the things I've been talking about here.

You can often see very young children experimenting with the effects of noises they've made and mimicking the noises they hear around them. Many toddlers aged between nine months and two years old will spend a good deal of time, especially at bed-time when they're on their own, doing long monologues of babbling sounds which mimic the cadences of speech and eventually progress into words. They are like sound poems or nonsense songs:

Bee bee bee boo baa bob bub bub bee bee mmmm mum mum mum mee mee ...

This is part of how a child develops their earliest vocabulary (words for things: mums, dads, carers, siblings, a pet's name, bottle, names for food and so on). One of my children's first words was 'Bob' – the name of the dog on the Welsh farm where we were staying. When these monologues progress to include words they can be quite amazing, as with the example I gave in Chapter 2 (Laura singing) where you can see and hear how three-year-old Laura is playing with phonology, syntax, morphology and lexis (sounds, grammar, the structure and meaning of words) all at the same time. This is crucially part of how a child builds up the grammar of the language. And it's play!

What's really interesting here is that some of the first grammatical things that children say are often 'incorrect'. You are reading this book, you clearly have an advanced understanding of the English language. When you put this book down to go outside, you might say to someone else in the room, 'OK, I'm going.' This simple structure of the subject, 'I', plus the verb, 'am going', is one of the key building blocks of the 'standard' form of English. A child will hear many variations of this structure on a daily basis. Sticking with our going-out scenario, the child may also hear 'We're going out now', 'Let's go', 'Do you want to go out now?', 'Nanna's going now' and many, many others. Yet the chances are that the very first way a young child will announce they are going out will be to say something like 'Me go'. But why, if learning how to talk is 'imitation' (as we often think) would they say this? Unless it's the dialect around them, a child will not hear anyone say, 'Me go'. So why say it? Because the child is learning through play. The child will have learned to think of that sound, 'Me', as being themselves. The child will have learned that people saying 'go' or going' happens when they are leaving or moving around. By saying 'me go' they follow the pattern or grammar of subject-verb together. The point is, though, that they've played with it to produce their own way of saying it. It's a bit like Lego! They're finding that fitting one brick next to another does a job. It doesn't matter in the immediate short term that it isn't exactly as the Lego plan says you should, and yet their improvised sticking-together works fine. 'Me go park'? You get taken to the park! Whoopeee!

Something else you can hear is very young children getting their word structures 'wrong'. They might say, 'I goed to the shops'. Putting '-ed' on the end of some words tells us that something happened in the past. ('I lifted up the baby', say.) The child who says, 'I goed' knows the -ed trick. He or she doesn't yet know that we don't do the -ed trick with 'go'. Almost certainly the child will have heard 'I went', but at the moment of wanting to convey the same idea, the child improvised (played?) with '-ed' and popped it on the end of 'go' . It's 'wrong' but in a way 'right'! It's one stage in the process of learning the very many and very complicated ways we have in English to express the idea that we did or thought or felt something earlier.

If you know any very young children – perhaps you're a parent, relative or friend – please have a go at recording or writing down the things that the children say. Share it with the family. Ask yourself how much of what they're doing is play. Then in a couple of years' time, when the child is talking fluently, compare what you've recorded with how they are speaking now. How did they get from one way of talking to the other? How did my stepdaughter get from 'prets' to 'breakfast', from 'diddits' to 'biscuits'? How did my son decide that 'Broxbourne Lido' was 'Boxbrains Lido', and why did he stop calling it that?

I'll finish this section with something I watched very recently on the 'front' in Brighton. There are some very low dome-shaped structures there that a small person can have fun running round or over. A girl less than three and older than eighteen months was running round the dome and singing. She had made up a song that went very simply, 'Round and round and round and round I go'. She had made up a tune for it and as she sang it, she hopped, strode and jogged exactly to the rhythm of the tune, putting her foot down heavily each time she sang the word 'round' and again at the end when she sang 'go'. She did it several times, changing it slightly as she danced. I thought about this: it looked self-made. Yes, perhaps parents or carers had done some round-and-round songs with her, such as 'Ring-a-ring of roses', but this had the hallmark of a song-and-dance routine that she had made up. But why? What's the point? What's it for? Clearly, it gave her pleasure. It was fun. But in terms of learning, what was she getting to know? What knowledge? She was learning how to move, learning how her body and voice work. Very important. When we are young, we have to learn where the edges of our body are when we move. We have to learn how our own personal bone and muscle system works. (I do a lot of performing, and I'm still learning about mine!) She was teaching herself rhythm and how the rhythm of language can match the rhythm of her body. This is not something that a small baby can do. She had reached another stage, and surely we can say that all this would stand her in good stead for now, for the next few months and perhaps for the rest of her life when dancing, singing, speaking and generally being confident. But – and this is a big but! – she was also treating the world as hers. This dome thing was hers to explore in her way through play. The dome wasn't an obstacle or something that was forbidden. It wasn't something that dominated her. She was exploring its possibilities through song, dance and play. In a way, she changed the dome – or at least what that dome meant for her. She was discovering the dominess of the dome! (This is a form of 'cognition' – how do domes work? They are roundy, but they are also up-and-downy. You feel this in your body when you run round and round them and up and down them.)

I cannot stress how important I think this is. Is the world something that we just accept? Or is the world something that we feel free and confident enough to explore and interpret, form our own views and opinions about? This girl definitely found out that she could play with the world and, through play, find out a little bit of how it works. And it was great fun to do.

It's Like Riding a Bike

They say you never forget how. I wonder why this is. Could it be because the muscle-and-bone memory, the ability to balance yourself, the interacting mental and physical adjustments, are all something that ultimately have to be learned by the individual through personal experience?

I often watch parents and older brothers and sisters in the park teaching young children how to ride a bike. Quite often I've tried a combination of things: putting my child on the saddle and holding the bike from behind or sharing the hold on the handlebars; calling out instructions and ideas – 'try not to put your foot down' (or the opposite: 'put your foot down whenever you feel the bike falling over') and so on; and sometimes I've just watched what happens and stood by with the plasters! The fact of the matter is that it's one of those things that you can only really learn from: a) recognising the feeling in your body of what it's like when a bike starts to get out of balance; and b) realising what adjustments you have to do to put yourself back in balance; while c) remembering that there's not much point in overdoing what you do to restore balance or you will get out of balance straight away again! The kindly person – or the unkindly person – teaching you how to ride your bike can't really teach this. They can suggest that you listen to your body and feel the balance. They can suggest the kinds of movements you might make to get back in balance (move the handlebars, lean slightly one way or the other), but in the end it's all about you getting to know what out-of-balance, in-balance and the effects of moving handlebars and leaning feel like in your bone-and-muscle system. No one can feel that for you. We can talk about what it feels like, but that's not the same as the actual in-body, in-mind feelings.

Several things arise from this: how do we learn this? And is it knowledge? Is it education? I think we learn this to a great extent from play – in particular, the aspect of play that encompasses trial and error and playing with different solutions. So how do we learn that mind-bone-muscle thing? We jerk the handlebars too far and fall off ... next time I won't push so hard. We try a few turns of the pedals. Ah! That worked, but very slowly I found I was leaning more and more to my right and the bike fell over. Next time I'll lean the other way.

All these thoughts and hundreds of others go on in a split second. There is constant relay going on between the mind, nerves, bones, muscles. There are the nerves of instruction ('motor nerves') and the nerves of perception – the ones that tell you what you're doing. Your mind has got to learn how all this interacts. You've also got a whole cloud of fears, worries, views of yourself as a person, that come in and out of the matter too.

Again – no matter what someone is 'teaching' you, the actual process has to be self-taught. The actual process is learned through trial and error. If you fear failure too much, you'll give

Challenge yourself
– THE LONG GAME!

Instead of sticking on the TV next time you're bored, here's a tool to help you do something different.

Take a load of lolly sticks and split them into two groups. Paint the ends of half of them green, and the ends of the other half red. Green means 'play outdoors', and red means 'indoor adventure'. Write an activity on each stick, and next time you're bored, pick one! If you fancy going outside, pick a green stick. If you want to keep a roof over your head, go for red.

Green stick ideas

- Go for a walk but it cannot be your 'usual route'.

- Make a daisy chain.

- Climb a tree.

- Hunt for a four-leaf clover.

- Go for a picnic after dark (remember torches or candles – and possibly a hot water bottle).

- Write your name using your footprints.

- Play Poohsticks.

- Go for a walk and spell out your name using the first letter of the car number plates you see.

Red stick ideas

- Bake a cake, but swap at least one of the ingredients for something unexpected; then decorate it to look like a famous art work.

- Go to an art gallery.

- Make the biggest drawing/painting/collage you can.

- Go to a museum.

- Marbling (you can use food colouring for this if you don't have inks).

- Make a mobile out of items in your house. (Cutlery? Toothbrushes? Cookie cutters?)

- Write a letter.

up. If you don't mind failing, you won't mind experimenting. Welcome to learning to ride a bike through play!

Education Through The Centuries

These kinds of questions about how play contributes to learning are at the heart of much debate around education, and have been for the last hundred years and more. But as long ago as 1689, in his *An Essay Concerning Human Understanding*, the Enlightenment philosopher John Locke suggested that children's 'gamesome spirit' might be harnessed in the service of learning. ('Gamesome spirit' – do you like that phrase?) He said, 'the chief art is to make all that they have to do, sport and play too.' Likewise, in the eighteenth century, people were still debating whether it would be possible to trick children into learning instead of simply making them repeat things and beating them until they got it right. In 1744 Mary Cooper, a printer, publisher and editor, produced a book called *Tommy Thumb's Pretty Song Book*. It's the world's second collection of nursery rhymes, the first being made by the same Mary Cooper, but having since been lost! Only two copies exist of this second volume, one of which is in the British Library, in London. (I love this sort of nerdy detail.) At the end of the collection there's a little rhyme:

The Child's plaything
I recommend for cheating

Children into learning
Without any beating.

And it's signed (as it were) by 'N. Lovechild'.

The joke here is probably that 'N' stands for 'Nurse' – meaning in this context 'Nanny', the woman looking after a child. And 'Lovechild' is, we can assume, a description of a state of mind rather than a real name! The little verse is very revealing. Even though it is only four lines long, it tells us of a whole philosophy: children can be 'cheated into learning' through the use of a 'plaything'.

The key word here is 'cheating' – telling us that the established view was that a 'proper' education was solely through a form of instruction backed up by corporal punishment, which was only banned in UK state schools in 1986. (Technically, it remained legal in independent schools until 1998.) I'm just old enough to have experienced this, at least some of the time. Getting things wrong in class at any point during a period covering several hundred years could be taken as signifying a mix of idleness, mischief and rebellion, or all three. This was seen as sinful, and the purpose of beating was to prevent it happening. Having fun while learning was therefore considered to be somehow cheating the system, as if enjoying the act of learning somehow devalued it. School wasn't supposed to be fun.

It was in this kind of context that the first theories of play developed: it was in the eighteenth and early nineteenth centuries that people like Johann Pestalozzi, Friedrich Froebel and Elizabeth Peabody began to offer theories in opposition to this prevailing opinion – particularly in relation to young children – and then from the late nineteenth century onwards people like Margaret McMillan and Jean Piaget developed these further towards an attitude that we find more familiar today. A brief run-through of what they pioneered gives us a sense of the history of 'play'.

Johann Pestalozzi was a Swiss educationalist, teacher and founder of schools – especially for the poor. He used the proceeds of his writing to finance the Yverdon Institute, a school in a castle, which, for a short time, was famous throughout Europe. It's thought that Pestalozzi coined the term 'kindergarten' (literally: children's garden, or garden for children), a word that carries the sense not only of a garden where very young children go to play and learn but also of a place where they, like plants, will grow. Pestalozzi observed the 'charm and variety' children showed in 'free play' and made the claim that its methods would result in 'freedom and independence' (as quoted in Joe L. Frost on Pestalozzi, in *A History of Children's Play and Play Environments*). This idea can be seen in the Romantic movement of the time, spanning roughly from 1800 to 1850; Romantic poets and writers extolled the freedom found in nature and, in turn, recognised the inherent kinship between children and nature. To be clear, Pestalozzi was very much in favour of instruction in education but didn't see this as incompatible with play – he was calling for a role for free play within education.

Friedrich Froebel studied and worked with Pestalozzi but broke away from him and founded the first kindergarten in 1837 in Germany. He designed specific materials – blocks, cubes, balls and cylinders – which, he said, should be handled, examined and counted in order to derive meanings from them – rather than their properties being dictated to the child by a teacher. Alongside this, specific activities were prescribed, such as paper-cutting, weaving, drawing, painting, threading and stringing, but within the remit of the activity the child was given free rein. The idea was that the designed objects would stimulate discovery and the activities would stimulate inventiveness. He wrote that play was the 'inner hidden natural life in man [sic] [...] It gives, therefore, joy, freedom, contentment, inner and outer rest, peace with the world. It holds the source of all that is good' (Froebel 1887, in Frost, *History of Children's Play*).

In his blueprint for education incorporating play Froebel talked of a mix of exploration of nature (caving, climbing trees and mountains, roaming the forests and growing plants) alongside inventing new forms using nature, such as building huts out of rocks and branches. This idea of bringing nature into play was extended into the play spaces of kindergartens and playgrounds. It should be said that Froebel was not entirely consistent on exactly how much freedom should be allowed the child. Should children be left to play as they want, or should adults show children what to build with their blocks? Either way, Froebel's influence on education – particularly of the under-fives – has been extensive, though there has been a consistent and continuous critique of the ideas, practice and outcome from those who believe that it is instruction and the clear transmission of knowledge that encourage and nourish development and freedom.

Elizabeth Peabody opened the first English-language kindergarten in America in 1860. She was also a prominent member of the Transcendentalist movement, probably the first female publisher in the United States (she printed three of Nathaniel Hawthorne's first books on her own press) and importantly, an activist, spent many years touring America propagating Froebel's ideas. With young children she advocated structured play in opposition to rote-learning, and she encouraged the children to experiment and play with materials, specifically in art. Her activism was hugely influential in the spread of kindergartens across the US and 'nurseries' or 'nursery schools' in the UK. Peabody argued for these to underpin the public (i.e., non-private) school system.

Margaret McMillan was born in the US to Scottish parents but migrated to Britain and became a political advocate for health and education of young working-class children at a time when it was much overlooked. In 1914 she and her sister Rachel opened an 'open-air nursery school and training centre' in Deptford, south-east London, for children from eighteen months to seven years. Again, the sisters worked with the theories and practice of Pestalozzi, Froebel, Peabody and others, believing that young children learned best through exploring and through activity. They gave a distinct role to free play, particularly through outdoor play and water-play, and held that it was through first-hand experience of the world that children would achieve their full potential.

Rachel McMillan died in 1917, but both sisters can be credited with having had a huge influence on how we view the whole notion of play and children under the age of five or six. This is partly because they combined theory, practice and political activism. On a personal note, I attended first a state nursery school (Tyneholme) and then a state nursery class (Pinner Wood Primary School, attached to a 'big' school) between the years of 1949 and 1951. Both of them bore the mark of the McMillans both in their architecture and in their curriculum. Both had wide doors which opened directly out into outdoor play spaces where we could run, climb and play with water, sand and big movable objects. In urban areas this idea of a space big enough for young children to run and climb according to their own wishes is not trivial. Many of my nursery pals came from living spaces or home environments where that wasn't possible – and the same is true for many children today. The kinds of activities that people with gardens or secure local parks take for granted – playing with water, sand and soil, finding earthworms, staring at the sky, kicking or throwing a ball, chasing, climbing, falling over on grass and the like – are not available to hundreds of thousands of children unless they are provided by kindergartens and nurseries.

Maria Montessori was the first Italian woman to qualify as a physician. She was also an educationalist and teacher who studied children and pedagogy, first developing her theories when working with children with learning disabilities, then putting them into practice in her schools for children in working-class areas of Rome. The first – Casa dei Bambini – opened in 1907. She emphasised the role of a child's spontaneous activity in education and personal development, and stated that an educator should carefully plan and create environments within which this could happen. Some of the activities she declared to be a part of education were derived

Bringing nature into play

Find your nearest wood or park and build a den. Fallen branches and rocks are great for the base structure, and ferns are excellent for weaving in and out of your branch structure and even produce a bit of rain proofing! Don't forget to decorate your structure with feathers, interesting leaves or flowers.

If you're feeling confident in your waterproofing, why not put it to the test? Stand in your den while a friend tips a bucket of water over it.

from real life – sweeping, wiping down tables, domestic tasks – and Montessori observed that when children are given choice about what to do and how to do them, they devote great concentration to the activities. This, she said, led to 'spontaneous discipline', and that phrase neatly contains the tension that educators recognise between free play and teaching a child to conform to what are felt to be society's needs. Montessori methods and Montessori schools can be found all over the world today.

Jean Piaget was an experimental Swiss psychologist and theorist of child development. Over his long life he produced and adapted complex and sophisticated models for children's overall development, the different ways in which children learn within these models and how children (and ultimately all of us) develop or construct ideas, thoughts, notions and theories. There isn't space to describe this elaborate set of ideas and its critiques, but, to briefly mention just one of Piaget's theories, he argued that teachers should create situations that stimulate a child's curiosity. For many years this has been interpreted as involving aspects of play: offering choice, inviting play as ways of exploring the nature of something before it is taught or instructed, inviting free questioning and then incorporating what the child already knows (of life, or that specific topic or subject) into the field of what is about to be learned. As with many theorists who become gurus and whose ideas become widely accepted, there have been severe critiques both of his research methods and the resulting theories. These battles are central to some of the controversies within education right now. We are living in a time when this is challenged by those who believe what is in effect the reverse: that you should start with the instruction, the delivery of knowledge, and the curiosity will arise from that.

While – thanks to the thinkers and innovators we've just met – play is now central to our understanding of very young children's development, this emphasis dwindles as children get older. Play is acknowledged as absolutely key to meeting the early years standards in the UK, for example, and school inspectors assess all childcare and learning providers on how far they facilitate play in their settings. As we've seen, play supports learning, self-regulation and a plethora of vital physical skills. It could be said that, through play in their earliest years, children naturally develop a 'growth mindset'. This is an idea introduced by US psychologist Carol Dweck, which says that our intelligence and abilities are not only innate but can also be developed through hard work and practice, that learning from mistakes instead of giving up develops resilience. However, as children get older, have you noticed how their opportunities for free play – chances to make 'safe' mistakes in play – get fewer and fewer? When we tell children to prioritise certain subjects or to focus on activities that will 'get you a job' or, I might add, when we expect everyone to develop at the same pace and in the same way, we risk instilling the opposite of playfulness – a 'fixed mindset'.

This contention is much opposed by some, and the matter is hotly debated. There will always be discussion about the best way to learn as we get older. Maybe it's possible to maintain a truly playful approach within certain constraints. The influential psychologist Daniel Willingham, for example, distinguishes between 'rote knowledge' (parroting information we don't understand) and 'inflexible knowledge' (memorising information but understanding its meaning). He says that inflexible knowledge is an important first step towards 'flexible learning', where you can understand, manipulate and indeed play with the information out of context. The implication is that, while we can learn many valuable skills from the very beginning purely through play, to learn algebra or history or chemistry perhaps, educators need to set the parameters, to provide us with the building blocks for our play. It's a fascinating conversation that will no doubt continue to play out (!) in the years ahead.

By way of a conclusion, I'll say this: no matter what any given school authority says, there is always a wide variety between schools, between systems and between ages of child being taught in school, as to what is play, whether we learn from play, how much we do or don't learn from play, what else is needed in order to learn the body of knowledge necessary to operate in the world. Meanwhile, outside of school, outside of education in its various institutions of schools, colleges and universities, people find ways to learn and play, play and learn, for themselves.

Outside School Hours

This brief run-down of a tiny few of the big names who have influenced how play has been regarded within education overlooks a major question: what do children do out of school?

A child's waking life consists of about 7 × 16 hours a week – roughly 112 hours.

Leaving aside some ten weeks' or so holiday time in English schools, the time spent in formal lessons (leaving out registration, free periods, breaks, after-school clubs) for most children in state day schools is about 5 × 5 or 5 × 6 maximum hours per week – something like 25–30 hours.

The huge discrepancy between these two figures has a direct bearing on how we figure the aim and purpose of play within formal education, and what its purpose is for the rest of the time, some eighty or ninety hours per week – plus that ten weeks or more on holiday. Or, indeed, in a society in which we place huge emphasis on consumerism, choice and the rights of the individual, how much influence or control do the adult carers have on the matter? For the past forty-three years (the time I've been parenting children and young people under the age of eighteen – my first was born in 1976, my last in 2004), I've been constantly struck by the discrepancy between how my children have organised their lives out of school and how it's been organised within school. It's almost has if they have each learned (though on many occasions resisted) the notion that they are in effect two different people: in one of these lives their thinking, living and 'doing' have been timetabled, overseen, disciplined and examined by forces way out of their control. In the other they have spent countless hours doing things by choice, within un-timetabled 'windows' of freedom, attached but not directly overseen and observed but not examined. In some ways, this has been very similar to the kind of childhood that my brother and I experienced. I often wonder about these long, long hours both in my life but also in my children's, and ponder on what I and my children learned in this time. After all, a good deal of it has been spent playing, 'mucking about', 'hanging out' and trying things out.

I was very lucky to have had parents who, as it happens, read their Froebel, Montessori and Piaget, and provided my brother and me with a great variety of experiences within which they gave us mind-boggling amount of freedom to explore and investigate. Though they were both teachers, they were both active proponents of the 'I don't know' principle! If you asked them questions, they often pretended they didn't know and invited us to see if we could find out – largely from books, as it was the pre-internet era.

They thought that encouraging curiosity and investigation in this way was incredibly important, rather than simply feeding me and my brother information. They were very keen that we should think beyond received wisdom. They played with what came over the radio waves at us. They argued with the programmes as if the broadcasters were in the room. A lot of playing is about not sticking to the rules that are given to us but trying out the untested and new ways of doing things instead. Many of the greatest leaps forward in the arts, sciences, technology, music – any discipline you care to name – were made when people pushed the boundaries of what was already known. And this is true not just for children.

Try this: some time this week pick something you have always had an interest in but not pursued, and follow it up. But don't do it in a way that you have usually done it. So if you usually go straight to Wikipedia, try another route – the library, a phone call to someone or, if it's appropriate, see if there's another way to view this bit of knowledge in the real world. Thanks to the internet, you can now find birdsong and bird-calls attached to the name of the bird. I've taken to imitating the birdsong – I'm not bad at whistling; it was something that I learned through play – and matching it up to the song sample on the internet. I practise the birdsong by playing with lips, tongue and breath till I think I've got it right.

My parents were both active 'doers' in the home – knitting, typing, dressmaking, tent-making, carpentry, decorating – and involved us in these as apprentices. Huge energy went into planning and carrying out camping and hiking holidays in Britain and France, and on these holidays every day was made up of hours of what the educationists call unsupervised 'free play' in woods, up hills, in rivers, caves, on beaches, in the sea, on farms, sometimes on our own, sometimes with a friend, sometimes in groups of older and younger children. I spent hours and hours building dams in streams. My main companion and boss in this was Mart. He went on to become one of the world's most famous experts in tectonics – the movement of the plates on the earth's surface. If he hadn't spent a lot of time guiding me in dam-building he might never have become Mr Tectonic. Alongside this, for any activity that my brother or I expressed an interest in, our parents would find ways in which it could be accommodated. We joined out-of-school clubs and associations where we sang, acted, did sports or collected rocks. While I spent hours exploring a local stream, my brother built more and more elaborate models. I'm only too aware that for millions of children this kind of extended, supported, diverse play just doesn't happen.

I don't think that schools can or necessarily should provide what my brother and I enjoyed. Most learning and play theory comes to us via the educationalists I've described, who worked within different forms of education and educational institution. Much less attention is given to what children get from all the other parts of their lives. Why is that? Why is the majority of a child's life less interesting or less important than the minority part? Or, when it does receive attention, is it largely in terms of what they don't get, get wrong or are deprived of. The world of youth work, adventure playgrounds, out-of-school clubs and associations and just hanging about must surely be at the very least – in hours alone – as important as school.

So, let's look at ourselves for a moment as out-of-school animals. I would argue that some of the best gifts that parents and carers can give our children are the powers of investigation, interpretation, invention and co-operation. They are my magic foursome. And, no matter what schools do or how they do it, we at home have the freedom in all those non-school hours to help foster these powers through play. I don't say this because I have run hours of psychometric testing in the controlled environments of a classroom, set alongside a 'control' group, measuring the effects of particular 'interventions' – it comes from my eighteen years of childhood and adolescence and forty-three years of parenting.

Making Space For Play

In this book I have tried to show some ways to change how you might think about play, as a way of knowing the world. I've explored some ways you might cultivate a more playful approach, in yourselves and with your children or your wider family. In many ways, play seems to develop qualities that we desperately need now, as rapid changes in society and technology make flexible thinking, resilience and adaptability more important than ever. Whether we're thinking about art, words, material 'stuff', ideas, or responding off the cuff, if we take a playful tack, this allows us to reinvigorate, create, innovate and learn in so many ways.

And yet, in the battle for ideas, time, space and money, we can ask some questions: what do we as a society actually do about play? What have you heard people say about play on TV? Have you seen articles in your local newspaper or heard people talking about, say, the provision of play spaces or play workers in your area? Have you heard people talking about playtime in schools being cut down? When you've met up with friends – perhaps you're a parent – have you talked with them about how children play, what toys to buy, what toys can you afford or should afford, or whether your children are spending too much time playing on their phones, computers and tablets?

How much money does it cost to give your children the space, time and facilities to play well?

In many ways, we seem to be squeezing play out of the schedules, institutions and spaces we provide for our children – and for ourselves. For instance, in 2014, it was reported that 35 per cent of UK primary schools were building classrooms in their yards and playgrounds. Both the school curriculum and the school testing systems in England have squeezed out the time available for the arts and free play. And an increase in the amount of time required to do homework squeezes time for play and the arts too.

There are political currents and attitudes behind this. In a press interview in 2013, the then UK Childcare Minister, Liz Truss, said many nurseries were filled with toddlers 'running around with no sense of purpose'. She stated, 'Free-flow play is not compulsory, but there is a belief across lots of nurseries that it is. I have seen too many chaotic settings ... where there aren't sufficiently qualified staff, and children are running around, we are not getting positive outcomes.'[1] Comments of this kind are common in educational debates and flag up a whole attitude to how we look after very young children.

This gives us a question: do we want our nurseries to be filled with staff under instruction or guidance and get rid of 'aimless',

---

1 Reported in *Daily Mail* (21 April 2013). As you might imagine, nursery staff were keen to point out that the nursery day is in fact timetabled to include a mix of free-flow play, play initiated by teachers through questions or games and indeed 'activities where the teacher is clearly leading'. They were also keen to point out that you can't have highly qualified staff unless you pay for their training and pay their wages. And you can't have nurseries if you are closing them and not building new ones.

'purposeless' play? Or do we need to think seriously about our attitude, outlook and ideas about childhood, learning and what education might be for? Who do we want our children to be? And even, do we want the kind of society that doesn't like this kind of play?

If we take Ms Truss's words for it, 'free-flow play' stands accused of being a partner-in-crime in the production of chaos. But what is 'free-flow play'?

I guess this book is full of suggestions for 'free-flow play'. It is also full of observations of 'free-flow play' that may well have led to all kinds of social and technological advances. It has suggested that when we know how to think using our powers of 'association' or 'analogy' or 'imagination' we are in fact equipping ourselves to understand and interpret the world. If we do it with others, we are finding out how to co-operate. If we do it for any length of time, we find out that we are not weak, powerless, passive receivers of the world but we can be makers and changers of that world. Those are my claims!

So, what kind of purpose and aim was Ms Truss hoping for?

Perhaps part of the problem in the battle for play is that its value and benefits are so tricky to record or report on in any neat figures or algorithm. Put another way, it's hard to measure the benefits. And, as some have asked, are we now living in a society that says, if you can't measure it, it has no value?

I work in a university where I supervise students researching themselves as they teach or introduce books to children and school students. Mostly, they are keen for children to become 'engaged' with reading. This is a very different kind of research from one that tries, say, to measure whether children are reading 'well' or 'comprehending'. My students are mostly trying to find out whether the children get hooked on books, whether they talk about the books they read, and help each other find books that they'll enjoy. Or they may want to investigate the kinds of conversation that children will have precisely at times when they're not under pressure to produce right and wrong answers. You could say, then, that my students (who are mostly teachers) are investigating how children play with books, play with reading, try out things with books on the principle of 'trial and error without fear of failure'. Back in the olden days when I was a child, we used to call it 'going to the library' or 'having a chat with my friend about the good bits in *Treasure Island*'.

So my students soon find that what they mean by 'research' is not a mass of figures that prove 'success rates'. Instead, they are trying to find out the nature and meaning of the very experience of playing with books: qualitative research rather than quantitative. They are asking questions like 'What is really going on in the intense chat, discussion and debate between three children looking at a challenging picture book about people on an island who behave aggressively towards a stranger?'

If someone comes along and starts to measure these children in terms of scores on a test paper which asks them for right and wrong answers only, it may well be that some children score highly, some score middlingly and some score low down, but it won't tell us much at all about what really matters to the child in question. It won't tell us much about the child who, let's say, used to think that reading books didn't matter – but now thinks it does.

So in these ways our thinking around play becomes a battleground for ideas – and politics. This thinking forces us to wonder about questions such as 'What is childhood for?' and 'How do children learn?' Does it push people in power or us into setting up a more rule-bound and 'traditional' approach, against 'aimless, purposeless, free-flow play'?

This rigid division of ideas goes back hundreds of years. You can find roots of it in the Reformation in Europe and the wars that followed. Yet I hope that part of what I've done in this book is to muddle this opposition between tradition and playfulness and show that 'play' in itself has a long – and illustrious – tradition and history!

Play doesn't just run about aimlessly while 'tradition' has a teacher being listened to who is structuring an activity. Again, as you may have noticed, this book about play is itself extremely 'structured'! Every book I've ever seen on play is 'structured' – full of ideas, laid out one after the other. And perhaps when you looked at my descriptions of play in this book, or you remembered your play activities, you thought that play itself has its structures too. I can't think of anything more structured than the games of home-invented football that I play with my son or my daughter picking up leaves to stick on her picture of a picnic.

So we've really muddled this long-standing division between play as chaos, disorder, riot, licentiousness, carnival, on the one hand, and 'learning', on the other, as rules, order, discipline, control, instruction. Yet this opposition is, as I've suggested, as old as the hills – or nearly. You can see it in Bruegel's painting *The Fight between Carnival and Lent*. You can read it in the great outpourings of fear and loathing from the Puritan preachers of the sixteenth and seventeenth centuries, in their attitudes to theatre, popular May festivals, the carnival election of a 'Lord of Misrule' during the annual 'Festival of Fools', and in the preachers' diatribes that talked of 'inordinate haunting of great multitudes of people, especially youth, to plays' in theatres, which they said led to 'frays and quarrels' and 'evil practices of incontinency in great inns having chambers and secret places adjoining to their open stages and galleries' (statement from the Common Council of London, 1574).

Such people spoke for a need for these public carnivalesque events to be replaced by people sitting down in rows in churches listening to preachers. In the words of John Northbrooke in *A Treatise against Dicing, Dancing, Plays, and Interludes* (1577): 'For the feast days were to this end instituted, that the people should assemble together, to hear (not plays) but the word of God.' These comments remind us of the long tradition of people in authority being extremely suspicious of play.

What does this very selective, very brief cultural history of the politics of play in relation to those in authority tell us today?

Well, ultimately, it's still our governments that decide the content of schooling, which has a direct impact on play during the school day, as well as how much we spend and allow for parks, open spaces and libraries – where safe and supervised play might happen. Such places are (or were) safe areas for children to play a mix of 'free' games and activities along with organised games. Anyone who has followed the debates about knife crime will have heard impassioned comments from youth workers describing how the kinds of interaction they used to have with young people in and around youth centres and leisure facilities has been drastically reduced. Why? What possible justification can there be for this? How could it be policy to take those facilities and that safety away from young people?

And I'll finish with the Arts

The arts are playful. I mean that when you are an artist of any kind – singing, dancing, writing, acting, any part of the arts really – the particular activity you're in will at times be very playful, experimental, full of trial and error. Yes, at other times we might describe it more as a kind of apprenticeship, learning, acquiring knowledge, practising the same thing or similar things over and over again. There are times, too, when the moments of experiment are 'frozen' into a pattern of activity that you might then go on to repeat. Anyone who practises any kind of art form will know, reading this, of other moments when there is a lot of playfulness which mingles with the hard grind of 'getting it right' or hard grind of repeating it in a way that works. Over the years, people have interpreted these differences within the arts as political, favouring the experimental over the repeated, or the other way round: despising the experimental and loving the repeated. These are the old divisions between 'avant-garde' and 'traditional' arts. In fact, a lot of the arts involve both experimental and traditional elements in the different phases of doing the work. It's up to you how much or how little of each you do.

But then, to do most arts, you need the time, resources and facilities – which is another political question! You need to have had a key moment in your life when someone was there to give you encouragement and show you that you are entitled to write or paint or make pots or dance or sing or indeed play about within any of these forms and others.

How do such moments come about?

I would suggest that the key moments come at home, school, college, youth clubs and in special encounters with friends. Some of these are chance – we don't choose the aunt who sings in church, and society doesn't lay that on for us, except that in a free society no one is likely to prevent that aunt from singing in church. Others, though, are provided by the state or by privately financed trusts and charities.

If you visit the largest, most well-endowed and – dare I say – most expensive of our private schools, the facilities for theatre, music and art are mind-blowingly superb. You realise that in places like this there are people in charge who are convinced that the play that goes on inside these facilities will benefit the young people's state of mind, personal development, sense of camaraderie, feelings, sense of self and confidence.

Why then are the arts being squashed, squeezed and eliminated from so much of state education? Why, with the cuts, should it be harder and harder for most schools to afford arts facilities, arts teachers and the free non-syllabus time for young people to play with musical instruments, form bands, paint and sculpt in art rooms and write poems?

Is that fair or right?

Michael Rosen is one of the best-loved figures in the children's book world, renowned for his work as a poet, performer, broadcaster and educational campaigner. His bestselling books include *We're Going on a Bear Hunt*, *Michael Rosen's Sad Book* and *Quick, Let's Get Out of Here*. His books for adults include *Good Ideas: How to Be Your Child's (and Your Own) Best Teacher* and his memoir, *So They Call You Pisher!* He was Children's Laureate from 2007–2009, and received the Eleanor Farjeon Award for services to children's literature in 1997. He is Professor of Children's Literature at Goldsmiths University of London. His book to help children (or anyone) write poems is *What is Poetry?*